STAINED GLASS MAKING BASICS

All the Skills and Tools You Need to Get Started

LYNN HAUNSTEIN

STACKPOLE
BOOKS

Guilford, Connecticut

Published by Stackpole Books
An imprint of The Rowman & Littlefield Publishing Group, Inc.
4501 Forbes Blvd., Ste. 200
Lanham, MD 20706
www.rowman.com

Distributed by NATIONAL BOOK NETWORK
800-462-6420

Photographs by Alan Wycheck Photography

British Library Cataloguing in Publication Information available

Library of Congress Cataloging-in-Publication Data

Names: Haunstein, Lynn, author.
Title: Stained glass making basics : all the skills and tools you need to get
   started / Lynn Haunstein.
Description: 2nd edition. | Guilford, Connecticut : Stackpole Books, [2019] |
   Includes bibliographical references.
Identifiers: LCCN 2018036215 (print) | LCCN 2018038748 (ebook) | ISBN
   9780811766838 | ISBN 9780811736527 (paperback) | ISBN 9780811766838
   (ebook)
Subjects: LCSH: Glass craft. | Glass painting and staining—Technique. |
   Glass painting and staining—Patterns.
Classification: LCC TT298 (ebook) | LCC TT298 .H3865 2019 (print) | DDC
   748.5028/5—dc23
LC record available at https://lccn.loc.gov/2018036215

Printed in the United States of America

CONTENTS

INTRODUCTION

THIS BOOK CONTAINS THE ESSENTIAL INFORMATION
and instruction that a beginner needs to know to create basic stained glass
projects.

The material is presented in much the same way as a series of workshops
on stained glass making. In fact, the hands-on approach here is based on the
successful, time-tested classes taught at Rainbow Vision Stained Glass, LLC in
Harrisburg, Pennsylvania, where thousands of students have begun their stained
glass journey.

As obvious as it sounds, you should begin reading from the beginning and
continue through the end without skipping around—each chapter in the book
builds upon information contained in the previous one. You should familiarize
yourself with workspace needs and stained glass safety before learning how to
cut glass or solder. The projects are arranged by increasing difficulty, and the
skills you learn in one section carry over in sequence to the next. The additional
patterns printed at the back of the book can be used in any order once you have
completed all of the detailed step-by-step projects.

Keep in mind that stained glass making, like any handcraft, takes time and
patience to learn. Mistakes are inevitable, but they will become less common
as you gain experience. Also, remember to take a step back and admire your
completed projects. Slight imperfections, obvious while working closely,
disappear when viewing your artwork as it is displayed.

Enjoy the journey as you embark on the adventure of creating stained glass art!

1
CREATING A GOOD WORK ENVIRONMENT

IF YOU ARE JUST BEGINNING TO WORK WITH STAINED GLASS, you will want to set up a dedicated work area. Your first concern should be a table or work bench that is a comfortable height to stand beside while cutting glass. Our tables are about 36 inches high, but find a height that works best for you.

It is not a good idea to cut glass on a hard wooden or metal surface. Look for a surface that will cushion the glass while you cut. In our photo, the gray surface is a Homasote board. This substance is made from recycled materials by the Homasote Company in West Trenton, New Jersey, and can be purchased at certain building supply centers. It is a firm surface but has just enough spring to it to allow for successful glass cutting. Push pins and nails can be used with the surface to hold projects together. Homasote is also a fire-resistant material, which makes it a great surface for soldering your projects. A section of Homasote can be used over and over again before needing to be replaced.

You will want to set up your work area where creating glass debris and using chemicals will not pose a risk to others. Children and pets should not have access to your work area for obvious safety reasons.

You may be using lead-based solder and framing materials while working on stained glass projects. Adequate ventilation in your work area is important for working with metals and chemicals used in the stained glass process. Refrain from eating, drinking, or smoking in your work area.

A good light source in your work environment is important. Make sure you have adequate light for all aspects of stained glass—from cutting the pattern through the polishing steps.

While working with stained glass, you will be producing chips and shards of glass. Frequent use of a brush and dustpan will keep your work area safer. A hand-held vacuum can also be a good way to clear glass debris from your work space.

A handy water source is an asset to any work area. This can be either running water from a faucet or water brought to your work space in basins. You will need to wash your glass pieces, wash chemical residue from your projects, and wash your hands often. Old towels are great for drying the projects or glass. You will want to have several of these nearby.

You will need an electrical source for any tools that require power, such as a soldering iron, an electric grinder, a vacuum cleaner, and any other power tools that may come in handy.

Consider how you will store your sheets of stained glass. They should be stored vertically for easy access, and for their safety. If you choose to lean glass against a wall, use something like cardboard under the glass to protect it from a hard floor surface. Old milk crates can be used to store small sheets of glass—again, store the glass vertically. Flat stacks of glass on a floor or table surface can be subject to breakage.

You will begin to accumulate a number of small hand tools as you develop your glass craft. A toolbox or caddy will be very useful to store these tools and keep them handy. The layout of your work area will develop as you discover which tools you use most often.

2
STAINED GLASS SAFETY

IT IS IMPORTANT TO KEEP YOUR SAFETY IN MIND when working with stained glass! Stained glass making requires your full attention. If you are tired or distracted, wait for a time when you can fully focus on your project. Remember that glass has sharp edges, and always handle it with care. Frequently use a bench brush to sweep glass shards away from your work surface and into a trash can. This will help reduce the risk of getting small cuts from debris. Never brush your hand across your work surface, as you will certainly nick yourself!

When handling larger sheets of glass, carefully grip the sheet by the top edge and hold it perpendicular to the floor. Move large glass pieces slowly so that they don't tap against any other surfaces that could cause them to break. Avoid carrying a large piece of glass horizontally, as it may crack from the strain. Never hold a sheet of glass over your head, and certainly do not try to catch a piece of glass that is falling. Just step back and let the glass go.

Wear proper clothing in your work area. Long pants and closed-toe shoes are recommended to protect your legs and feet. Wear protective gloves when working with any harsh chemicals such as patina, which could irritate your skin. Always wear protective safety glasses or goggles when cutting or grinding glass, even if the task takes only a few seconds.

Keep a supply of adhesive bandages handy for small nicks and cuts that are virtually unavoidable when working with glass. A first aid kit containing antiseptic, gauze pads, butterfly bandages, and similar supplies is a good idea to have within easy reach, just in case you get a deeper cut.

Prevent children and pets from entering your work area. Carefully store all chemicals out of their reach.

When soldering, always use a heavy-duty soldering iron stand to hold your iron. Never place your soldering iron directly on your work surface, where it could be accidentally bumped or roll off your table. Always solder in a well-ventilated area, and do not inhale the fumes produced by hot flux and solder. Read the labels on these products for additional safety information.

You must use care when working with came and solder containing lead. As a general rule, stained glass hobbyists are exposed to very low levels of lead while creating their projects. However, any time lead is present in the environment, it should be handled and used responsibly. Prolonged exposure to high levels of lead can pose significant health risks.

Here are some ways to keep lead exposure to a minimum:

- Pregnant or nursing women should avoid contact with all stained glass materials containing lead.

- Never eat, drink, or smoke while working with lead.

- Wear the same work clothes each time you are working with lead. Keep these clothes in your work area to prevent lead dust from being carried into your living space. Wash these work clothes separately from other laundry items.

- Wash your hands frequently while working with lead, but especially before leaving your work area.

- Keep your work area clean to prevent tracking any lead particles into your living space.

- Always recycle your lead scraps responsibly.

Using common sense while creating stained glass projects will go a long way toward keeping you safe and healthy while you enjoy your craft.

3
TOOLS AND SUPPLIES

TAKE SOME TIME TO LEARN ABOUT THE MATERIALS and equipment needed for successful stained glass making. Some of the items listed on the following pages might be in your toolbox or workshop right now. Other, more specialized tools need to be purchased at your local stained glass shop. Each project in this book requires a different combination of the equipment and materials explained in this section. A supply list is included at the start of each project, specifying all the tools and materials you will need to complete it. This list can be copied and taken along to the store with you when you go shopping.

PAPER PACK: OAK TAG, CARBON PAPER, AND TRACING PAPER

Oak tag
This paper has a thickness and texture similar to a manila file folder. It is used to make patterns to build your projects on.

Carbon paper
This is the inky blue or black paper used to transfer the pattern of the project onto oak tag paper.

Tracing paper
This very thin paper is translucent and allows the lines from the original pattern to show through so they can be traced.

DRAWING TOOLS

Keep a supply of pencils and markers on hand for drawing patterns, color-coding, and marking the glass.

RULER

This is used as a measuring tool and to make straight, even lines while drawing or cutting. A ruler backed with cork or other skid-resistant material is a good choice.

CUTTING SQUARE

Used much like a ruler, the cutting square is designed to gauge straight lines based on a right angle, which is helpful when drawing shapes such as squares and rectangles. A raised lip along the underside of one edge of the square keeps it from moving when you're cutting a right angle.

PATTERN SHEARS

These special scissors are designed so the single top blade fits inside the double blades on the bottom, delivering a cut that removes a thin strip of paper. This strip is important for stained glass making because it allows room for the copper foil or lead between pieces of glass so that your project fits together perfectly. Typically, shears are available that leave a 1/32-inch gap for foil-edged projects and a 1/16-inch gap for lead projects, as you can see in the photo here.

Some manufacturers produce a model of pattern shears with interchangeable blades for working with both copper foil and lead. It is also a good idea to keep a regular pair of scissors nearby for routine cutting and trimming.

RUBBER CEMENT

This is used to glue paper patterns onto pieces of glass prior to cutting.

SAFETY GLASSES

These should be worn for eye protection while breaking or grinding glass.

BENCH BRUSH

A sturdy brush is perfect for sweeping shards of glass from the work area into a trash can to eliminate the risk of injury.

HOMASOTE BOARD

This board makes a great work surface when cutting glass, pinning projects into place, and soldering.

GLASS CUTTERS

A quality glass cutter is the most important tool a beginner must have before starting a project. All cutters consist of a handle and a metal wheel of some type that turns against the glass to create a weakened seam called a *score*.

The metal wheel, which rotates much like a pizza cutter, is not sharp to the touch. It must be lubricated before each cut to reduce friction between the blade and the glass.

Some cutters require manual lubrication, whereas the higher quality ones are self-lubricating.

Keep in mind that learning to use a cutter correctly takes some patience and practice, as the tutorials in chapter 5 will demonstrate.

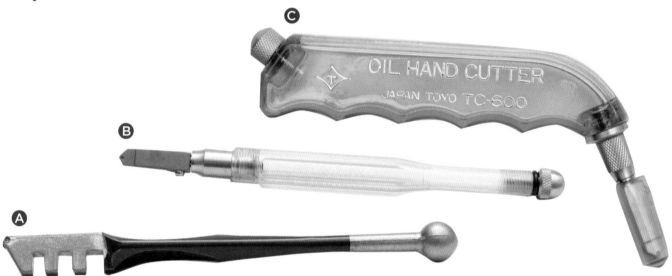

Ⓐ *Traditional steel wheel cutter*

The most inexpensive and "low-tech" of all cutters, this type uses a rotating wheel of honed steel to score and weaken the surface of the glass before breaking. The wheel must be manually lubricated before every cut to reduce friction on the glass that might shatter or chip it. The grip typically is made of metal, plastic, or wood and is designed to fit well in the hand. Most have a weighty ball on the back end of the grip for tapping scored glass, and three indentations near the tip that can break or chip glass if needed.

Ⓑ *Pencil grip cutter*

This quality cutter uses tungsten carbide, a very hard metallic element, in the cutting wheel. This makes it more durable than the steel type and allows it to cut much more efficiently and with much less force.

The plastic handle of the cutter serves as a reservoir for the oil that lubricates the cutting wheel. The grip is designed to fit comfortably in the hand, and the tip on this cutter can last a very long time.

Ⓒ *Pistol grip cutter*

This variation of a tungsten carbide wheel cutter replaces the simple shaft of the pencil grip with a pistol grip for easier and more precise handling. The handle is hollow and holds the glass cutting oil, which flows from the reservoir down to the wheel through a small tip containing an absorbent wick. The oil from this wick allows for continuous lubrication while scoring the glass.

Many stained glass hobbyists prefer this kind of cutter because it helps reduce some of the hand fatigue that might occur with a standard cutter, and it allows greater control while cutting the glass.

CUTTING OIL

A number of manufacturers sell oil specifically designed for use with glass cutters. The oil helps to reduce friction between the cutter wheel and glass surface, and it also helps to keep small flecks of glass from impeding the rotation of the wheel.

GROZING/BREAKING PLIERS

These stained glass–specific pliers are used for two purposes. As a breaking plier, this tool is used with the flat side facing upward to grip and break off curved or narrow pieces of glass that have been scored.

As a grozing plier, the curved side faces up while chewing or grinding away small points of glass.

RUNNING PLIERS

These pliers are used to carefully break a piece of glass along a straight score line. The top jaw of the pliers is flat, while the bottom contains a narrow, raised section in the center of it. This raised section is positioned under the score line. When the pliers are squeezed gently together, the force causes the glass to break evenly along the score. These are especially helpful when cutting long strips of glass.

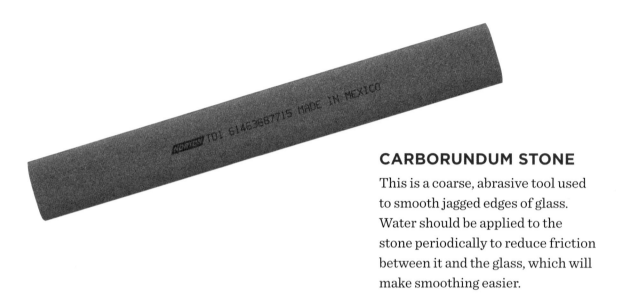

CARBORUNDUM STONE

This is a coarse, abrasive tool used to smooth jagged edges of glass. Water should be applied to the stone periodically to reduce friction between it and the glass, which will make smoothing easier.

GLASS GRINDER

These grinders take the place of the Carborundum stone and instead use a rotating wheel to smooth sharp edges of glass. They are designed to be used on the tabletop, and most feature an eye protection guard and a small, water-filled chamber that keeps the grinding wheel cool during operation.

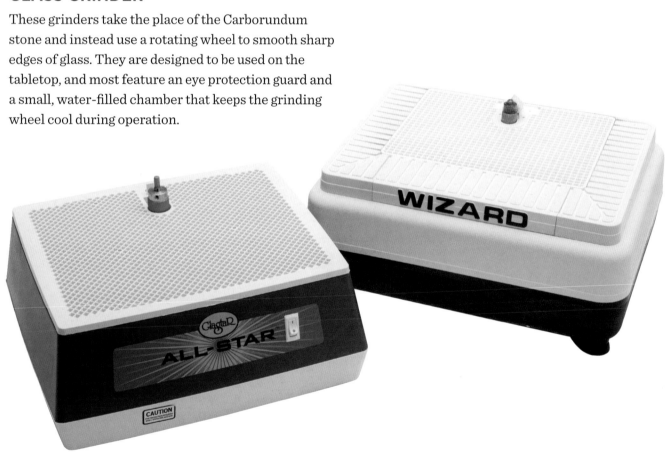

COPPER FOIL

This shiny foil tape is applied carefully to the edge of a cut piece of glass and wrapped so that it covers a portion of both sides of the glass. It provides a surface to which solder can bond. Most foil sold for stained glass making comes in rolls and is backed with adhesive for easy application. Popular widths are 3/16 inch, 7/32 inch, and 1/4 inch; 7/32 inch is standard for most projects.

Copper foil comes backed in three colors: copper, black, and silver. The foil backing you use should match the patina of your finished project.

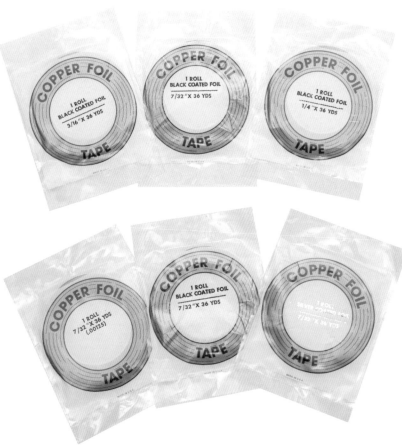

FOIL DISPENSER

A copper foil dispenser can make foiling easier and more efficient. Foiling by hand is recommended for beginners until the technique is well understood.

HAND FOILER

A hand foiler can be used to work more efficiently as well. It separates the protective paper from the foil and aids in centering the glass.

FOILING MACHINE

A foiling machine is also a great tool to use. When used properly, it can reduce the time it takes to complete this step by half. The machine helps center the foil on the glass and begins to fold the foil over the edges of the glass.

CRAFT KNIFE

This is the perfect tool for correcting mismatched overlaps of copper foil.

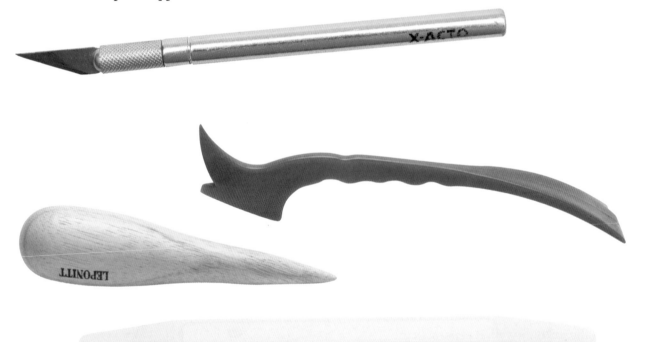

FIDS (WOODEN OR PLASTIC)

This tool comes in a number of shapes and sizes and is used mainly as a burnishing or smoothing tool when applying foil to stained glass. It also can be used to gently pry open the channel portion of a piece of lead came.

LEAD CAME

These are long strips of pliable lead, usually sold in six-foot lengths, which make up the entire framework for leaded glass projects. They have a central channel to hold pieces of glass in place, provide the metal surface needed for soldering, and establish the lines and curves that define a project.

As shown in Figure 1, most types of came have channels that are either H-shaped (pictured on the left) for holding two pieces of glass along a shared edge, or U-shaped (pictured on the right) for holding a single piece of glass along an outside edge.

Figure 2 shows a variety of sizes of U-shaped channel lead on the left, and two sizes of H-shaped lead on the right.

Note: Refer to chapter 2 for information about the safe handling, use, and storage of lead materials.

OTHER METAL CAME

Pieces of brass, copper, or zinc are used in projects that require a very sturdy and rigid material. These are also available in both H-channel and U-channel varieties.

LEAD VISE

This simple metal vise is used to hold a strip of lead came in place so that it can be stretched before use. Stretching came makes it straighter and stronger.

LEAD CUTTERS

Lead cutters, also called lead dykes, have blades that are flat on one side and concave on the other. They are used to cut lead came, making a variety of straight or angled cuts.

LEAD KNIFE

This tool can also be used to cut lead came cleanly.

LEAD BOARD WITH RIGHT ANGLE

This board, made of plywood and wood strips, is used to hold the side and bottom of a lead project in place while it is being put together. It is also useful when framing a copper foiled project. A lead board needs to have a precise 90 degree angle built into the lower left corner.

HORSESHOE NAILS

These long, narrow nails are flat on one side, making them perfect for holding lead came in place during project building.

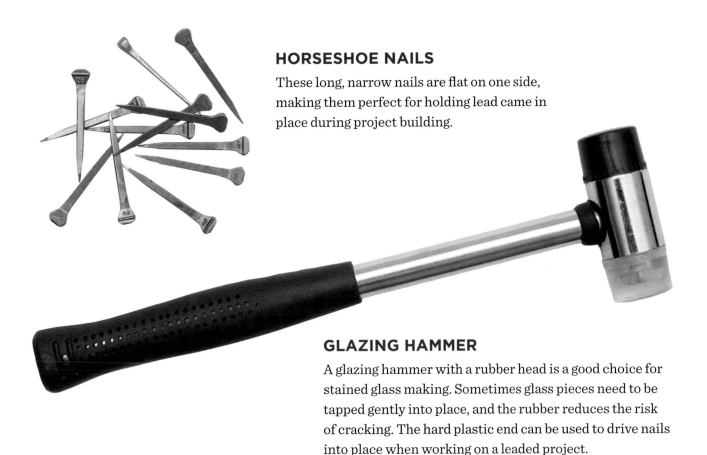

GLAZING HAMMER

A glazing hammer with a rubber head is a good choice for stained glass making. Sometimes glass pieces need to be tapped gently into place, and the rubber reduces the risk of cracking. The hard plastic end can be used to drive nails into place when working on a leaded project.

FLUX AND BRUSH

Flux is a mild acid used to clean oxidation and other dirt from metal surfaces so that melted solder will adhere readily. Without flux, solder would simply not flow over the copper-foiled edges of glass or on lead. Flux can be found in liquid, gel, or paste form, and each works well for foil and lead projects. Because it is corrosive, be sure to wash flux from your project as soon as you are finished soldering.

Any medium-to-firm brush designed to apply paint or solvent-type materials can be used to apply flux to a project.

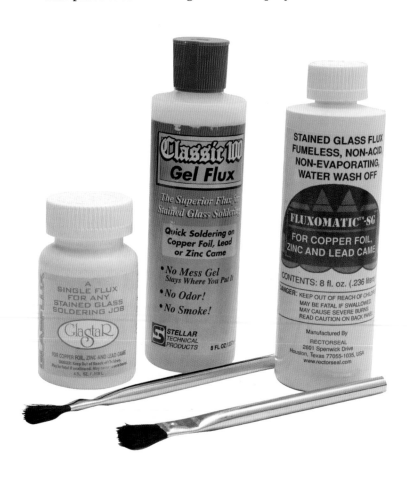

SOLDER

The solder used in stained glass making is an alloy of tin and lead that is melted with a hot soldering iron and applied to pieces of metal or foiled glass to bond them together. The most common solders are sold in coiled spools and are available with either a 50-50 ratio of tin to lead or a 60-40 ratio of tin to lead. The 60-40 solder tends to flow more smoothly and is typically easier to work with than the 50-50 blend. A no-lead solder is also available and is generally used in jewelry making.

SOLDERING IRON

The soldering iron is used to melt solder, which joins two or more pieces of copper-foiled glass or lead together. A number of models come equipped with an adjustable control on them for maintaining a specific temperature; other models can be plugged into a separate rheostat unit and have their temperature adjusted in that way. Another type of iron uses interchangeable tips to regulate temperature.

SOLDERING IRON STAND

A sturdy stand is recommended for convenience and safety. The stand usually consists of a heavy, stable base with a coiled piece of metal attached for holding the iron when it's not in use. This helps prevent accidental burns and keeps the iron from being dropped or knocked to the floor.

Most stands typically have a small tray in the base where a moist sponge is placed for periodically wiping solder and flux residue off the hot iron.

IRON TIP CLEANER (SAL AMMONIAC)

Sal ammoniac is a naturally occurring or man-made mineral composed of ammonium chloride that reacts to the heat of a soldering iron and helps clean residue from it when the iron is gently scraped across it.

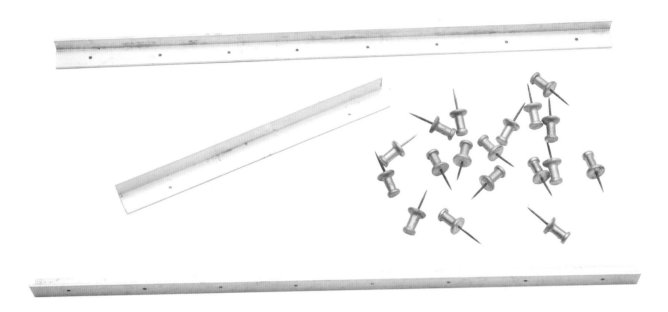

LAYOUT STRIPS AND PINS

These items can be used to make a jig to hold your project in place while you are working on it.

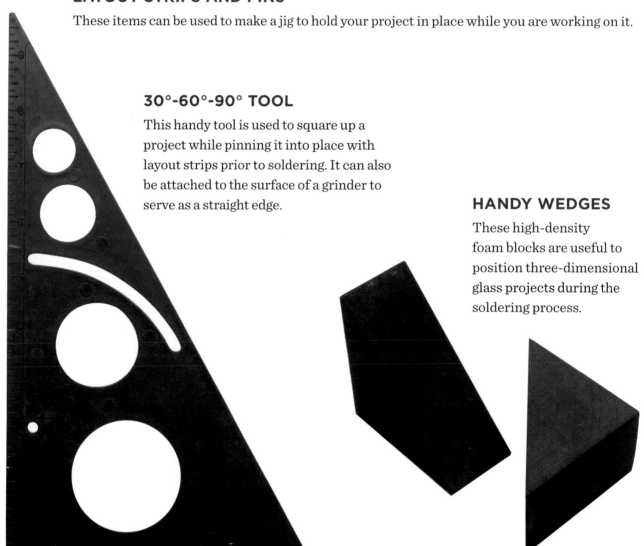

30°-60°-90° TOOL

This handy tool is used to square up a project while pinning it into place with layout strips prior to soldering. It can also be attached to the surface of a grinder to serve as a straight edge.

HANDY WEDGES

These high-density foam blocks are useful to position three-dimensional glass projects during the soldering process.

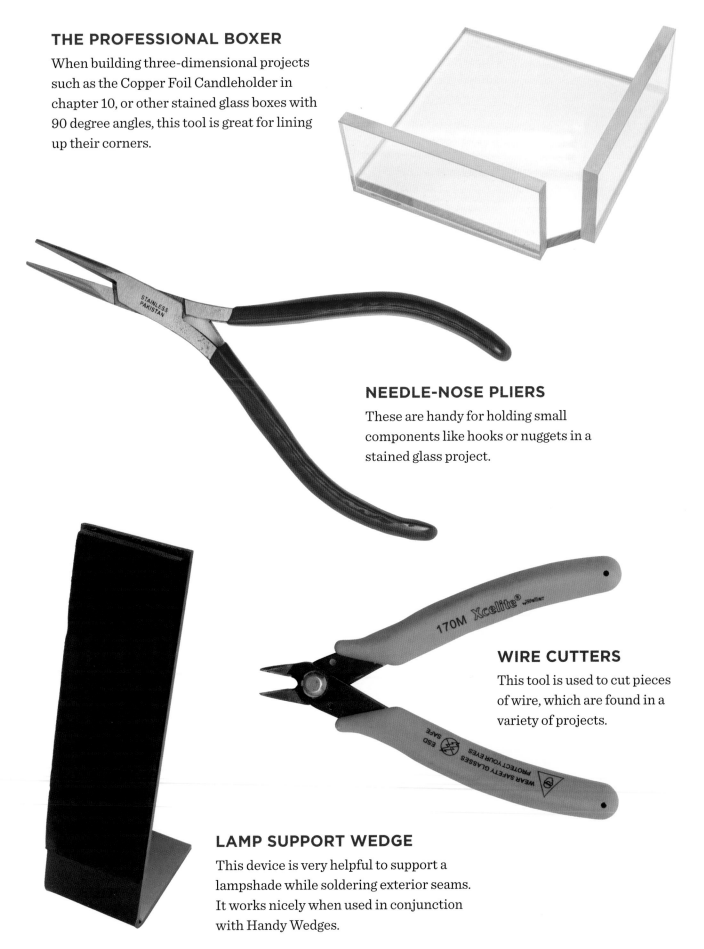

THE PROFESSIONAL BOXER

When building three-dimensional projects such as the Copper Foil Candleholder in chapter 10, or other stained glass boxes with 90 degree angles, this tool is great for lining up their corners.

NEEDLE-NOSE PLIERS

These are handy for holding small components like hooks or nuggets in a stained glass project.

WIRE CUTTERS

This tool is used to cut pieces of wire, which are found in a variety of projects.

LAMP SUPPORT WEDGE

This device is very helpful to support a lampshade while soldering exterior seams. It works nicely when used in conjunction with Handy Wedges.

PRE-TINNED COPPER WIRE

This wire can be used to make hooks or reinforce stained glass projects, adding stability and strength.

HOOKS AND CHAIN

You can choose from a variety of hooks, chain, and rings for hanging and displaying finished stained glass pieces.

MILD DETERGENT

A mild detergent should be used during the cleaning stages of your projects.

FLUX AND PATINA NEUTRALIZER

This substance neutralizes chemicals in flux and patina and will need to be applied at the end of most projects.

PROTECTIVE GLOVES

These should be worn when working with patina and other chemicals.

PATINA

Patina is a liquid solution that changes solder and other metals from silver to black, dark gray, or copper. Patina contains chemicals that are harmful to the skin and lungs, so it must be used with care and caution.

A stained glass piece should be rinsed with warm, soapy water after the patina is applied to neutralize the chemical reaction and make it safe to handle.

STAINED GLASS POLISH

Applied as the last step of a copper foil project, this finishing compound will polish the glass and metals and help slow the oxidation process.

TOWELS

A variety of old towels are handy to have in your workshop for cleaning and polishing your projects.

GLAZING CEMENT

This material is applied to a leaded stained glass project to seal and strengthen the joints formed by lead came. The putty, which typically comes packed in linseed oil, must be mixed well before use.

WHITING

Whiting is a white powder, typically composed of calcium carbonate, which is used to dry the glazing cement and allow it to set. Whiting also helps clean excess putty from the glass surface.

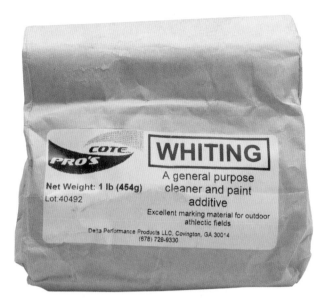

BRUSHES FOR LEAD WORK

A stiff-bristled brush about 6 inches wide is used for applying glazing cement. A second brush should be used to work the whiting into the cement.

STEEL WOOL

A superfine grade of steel wool can be used to remove oxidation from solder and other metal parts.

4
UNDERSTANDING GLASS

GENERALLY SPEAKING, MOST STAINED GLASS IS CREATED when a mixture of sand, ash, metal oxide colorings, and other ingredients is heated to very high temperatures until it becomes a molten liquid. This liquid is then either blown or rolled into solid glass sheets and allowed to cool. This process can occur either by hand or with the help of machinery; each technique can significantly alter the appearance, texture, and price of the glass.

CLEAR TEXTURES

Clear textured glass is often used in cabinet doors, but also serves a variety of functions in traditional stained glass projects. It can be used as a background for panels and in three-dimensional projects like the candleholder in chapter 10.

The following examples are of different clear textured glasses, shown in front of a black background to enhance their appearance in the photos.

Baroque

Seedy

Glue Chip

Crackle

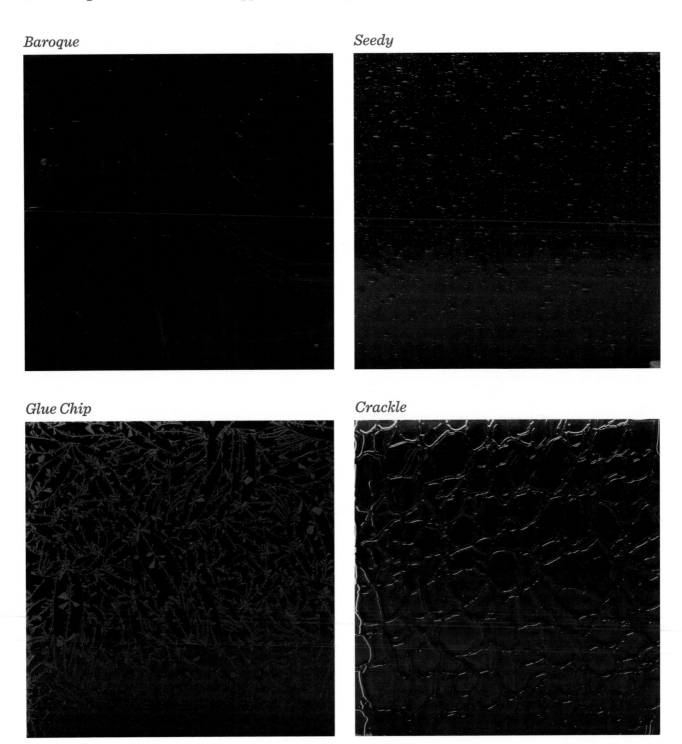

STAINED GLASS

Stained glass generally falls into one of two categories: cathedral or opalescent.

CATHEDRAL GLASS

Cathedral glass is very transparent, meaning that light passes through it easily. This kind of glass is perfect for many stained glass projects, such as those designed to hang in a window or be backlit by another light source. Cathedral glass is made in many colors and textures, and most are great for beginners to use because they are fairly easy to cut.

The following are some examples of cathedral glass:

Teal Waterglass

Green Rough Rolled

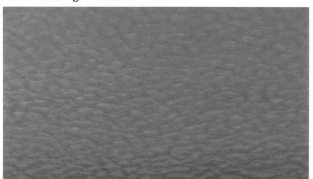

Sky Blue Wispy

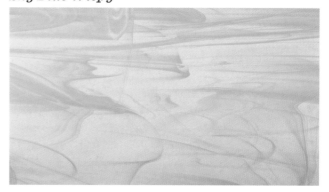

Red Ripple

Yellow Wispy

Red and Amber Waterglass

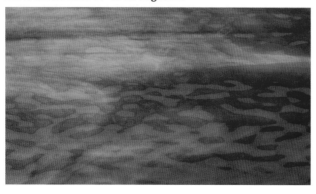

Clear/Blue/Purple Streaky

OPALESCENT GLASSES

Opalescent glasses, also referred to as opals, don't transmit as much light as cathedral glass because the glass has a milky, dense quality to it. Most opals are considered semitranslucent, meaning they allow some—but not all—light to pass through. Some opals are virtually opaque and allow no light to penetrate at all.

The following are some examples of opalescent glasses:

Brown/Red/White/Clear Corsica

Aqua/Lime/White/Clear Corsica

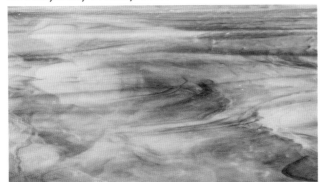

Black Waterglass

Purple/Green/Blue/White Streaky

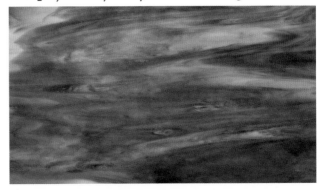

Dark Rose/White Streaky

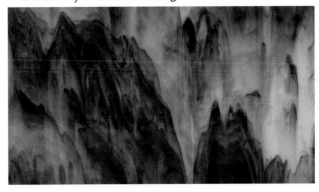

Brown/Green/White Streaky

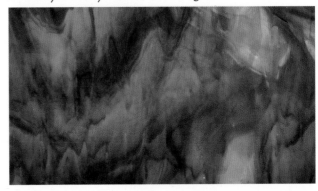

Deep Blue/Green/White Streaky

IRIDIZED GLASS

Iridized glass has a shimmering surface, which may be found on select cathedral or opalescent glasses.

Iridized Krinkle

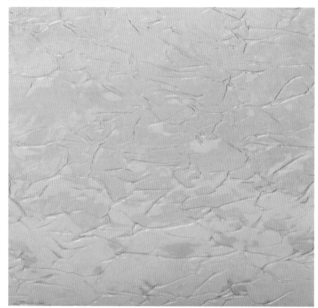 

Iridized Blues

ART GLASS

Another subcategory of glass is art glass, which may be blown or hand-rolled and often blends cathedral and opalescent glasses together. This glass may be more expensive than traditional stained glass, but it creates beautiful lamps, panels, and windows.

Blue/White/Green/Pink Streaky Granite

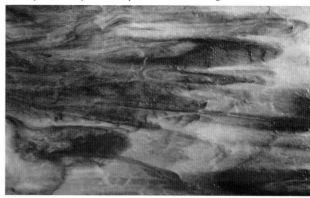

Deep Green/Ice Stipple

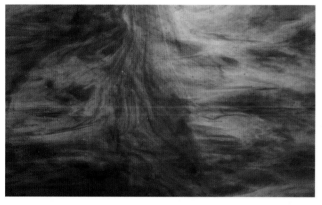

Pink/White/Clear Baroque

Pink/White Reproduction Glass

Multicolored Streaky Opalescent

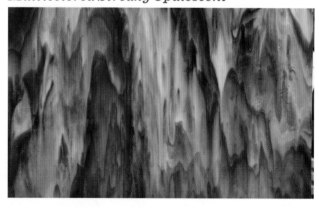

Amber/Green/Blue/White Streaky Granite

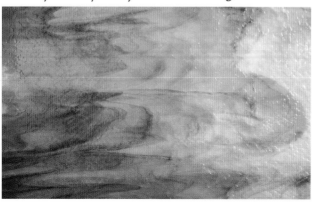

Fracture and Streamer

ACCESSORY GLASS

Glass components may complement sheets of stained glass in a variety of projects. As you become more familiar with these products, you will find there are endless possibilities to enhance your stained glass creations.

NUGGETS

These are smooth, rounded drops of glass with flat bottoms. One example of how to incorporate nuggets into a project is shown in the Bevel Star with Glass Nuggets in chapter 9.

FACETED JEWELS

These are pieces of glass that have been manufactured to simulate precious stones. They have many facets that catch the light, adding an extra sparkle to any project.

BEVELS

Bevels are precut pieces of glass with angled edges. They refract light somewhat like a prism and can create rainbows of color when sunlight shines through. Bevels are used to create both bevel star projects in chapter 9 and are also highlighted in the Copper Foil Candleholder in chapter 10.

5
BASIC GLASS CUTTING SKILLS

FOR MOST PEOPLE, THEIR FIRST GLASS CUTTING EXPERIENCE can be rather intimidating. Some may be concerned that the glass will shatter into many pieces, while others will be wary of cutting themselves with sharp glass edges. In reality, glass will break easily along your score lines if you take the time to learn the proper techniques. While it is possible to nick your fingers when cutting stained glass, careful handling of glass and its scraps will keep those events to a minimum.

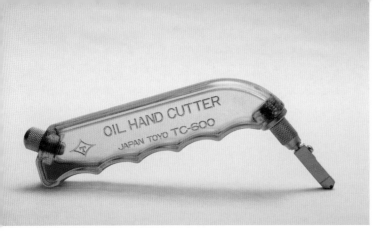

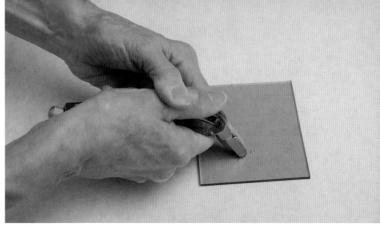

We use the term *glass cutting*, and we use a tool called a glass cutter, but in actuality we are simply scoring the glass. This means we scratch the surface of the glass with our cutter; then we break the glass using either our hands or a tool. Glass is created by mixing sand, or silica, with other minerals, and heating them to a very high temperature. When the glass has been properly cooled, you can separate the microscopic particles on the glass surface using a tungsten carbide cutter wheel. Your score line creates a weak point in the glass that can be easily broken using the methods described in this chapter.

Learning proper scoring and breaking techniques is one of the most important steps in stained glass work. As you develop good skills in this area, you will find that the quality of your other stained glass skills will also improve. Accuracy in each step will lead to the completion of quality art glass projects.

HOLDING A GLASS CUTTER

TRADITIONAL STEEL WHEEL CUTTER

One option is the traditional wheel cutter. If using this tool, you will need to dip it in cutting oil every few scores. To hold this style of cutter, place it between the first two fingers of your dominant hand and grasp the shaft of the cutter with your thumb and forefinger.

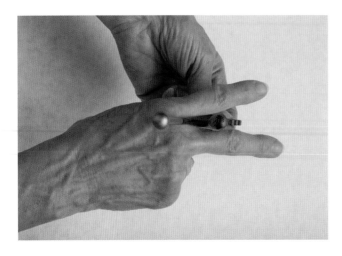

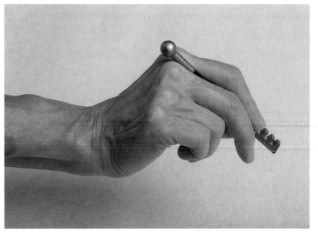

Place the thumb of your non-dominant hand on top of the cutter and your index finger along the cutting wheel. This style of cutter is used while scoring the glass toward your body.

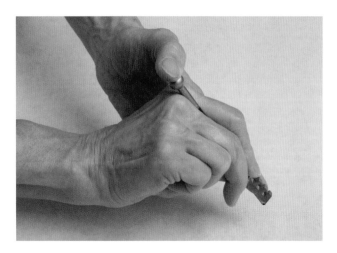

PENCIL GRIP CUTTER

A pencil grip cutter with an oil-fed tip can also do well for scoring stained glass. Hold the cutter in your dominant hand like a pencil and use your nondominant hand to help guide the cutter head. When scoring the glass, you will cut in the direction moving away from your body.

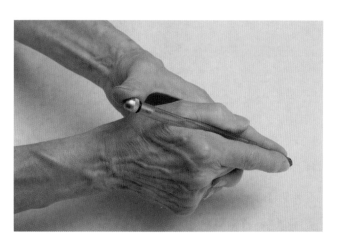

PISTOL GRIP CUTTER

One of the most comfortable glass cutters is the pistol grip style. It fits nicely in your hands, and can be easily guided along the glass. Because of its design, even a beginner can cut glass for quite some time before developing any hand fatigue.

To hold a pistol grip cutter, hold it in your dominant hand and wrap your nondominant hand over the top. Extend your index finger from your nondominant hand down along the cutter wheel, which will guide it as you score the glass. When scoring the glass with this style of cutter, you will cut away from your body.

SCORING THE GLASS

For safety, put on protective glasses. When cutting glass, you'll want to set up your work area with a work surface, such as Homasote. This material will protect your work space, as well as provide a nonrigid surface that will have just a bit of give to it.

Stand up so that you are in a better position over the glass. Holding the pistol grip cutter as described above, make sure that the barrel of the cutter is parallel to your work surface.

Start with the cutting wheel up on the edge of the glass and glide with continuous pressure toward the opposite side of the glass.

Here you can see a good score and a bad score; one that is too heavy chips the glass. The one on the bottom is just right.

Just before reaching the other edge of the glass, lift the cutter about 1/16 of an inch from the edge so that the cutter head doesn't chip the glass.

Notice that if you run the cutter over the edge when completing the score, the glass is likely to chip.

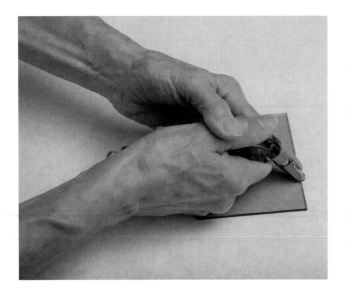

CUTTING PRACTICE

To begin your glass cutting session, assemble some scraps of glass. Window glass can be an inexpensive material to begin with that is also fairly easy to cut. You will want ten or twelve pieces of glass, cut into 3- or 4-inch squares to practice your skills.

Put on your safety glasses.

Take a square of practice glass and draw three straight lines on it with a permanent marker. Score the middle line first, centering the notch of the cutter wheel on the marker line. Remember to lift up just before you reach the opposite edge.

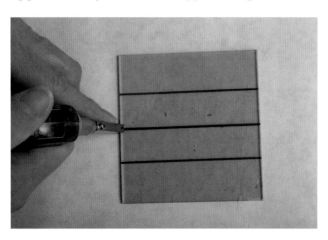

The easiest way to break a piece of glass is with your hands. Put your thumbs on either side of the score line at the base of the score, and curl your fingers underneath.

Push up with your fingers to break the glass.

On a remaining section of glass, make a second score following the marker line.

Here are grozing pliers. Notice that the bottom jaw is rounded and the top jaw is anvil shaped. To break the glass, keep the anvil side up.

Bring the pliers in perpendicular to the score line at the base of the score, with your thumb on the opposite side. With the pliers and your curled fingers underneath, push up with your fingers to break the glass.

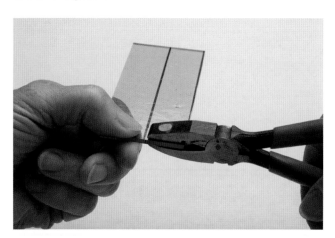

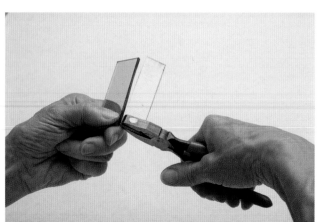

Make a third score and break this one with the running pliers. These running pliers have a line on the top to indicate that side faces up when breaking glass. Inside the pliers there is a bump that provides the leverage for breaking the glass.

Place the glass in the jaws of the running pliers so that the marking aligns with the score. The glass should sit in the jaws of the pliers about a quarter of an inch.

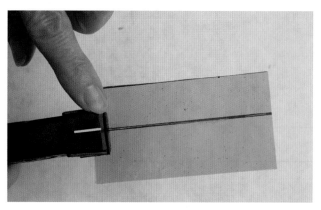

A gentle squeeze with the pliers will break the glass.

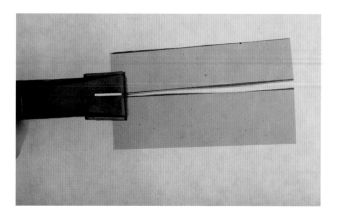

Here are basic cuts.

Now it's time to practice cutting some shapes. Refer to chapter 13 for patterns of the practice shapes.

SHAPE #1
This is a simple trapezoid.

To cut out this shape, start at the edge of the glass, follow the design, and go to the opposite edge of the glass. Score and then break that line using your hands.

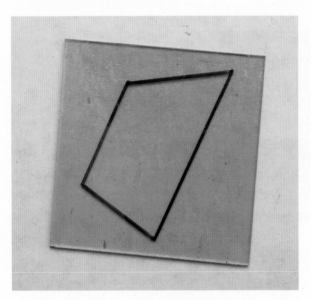

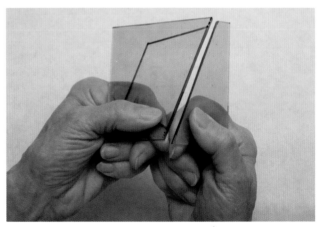

Now score the next side and continue to the opposite edge. Break that off with grozing pliers, remembering to position the pliers at the base of the score, perpendicular to the score line.

Score the third side, continuing to the opposite edge of the glass. Break the score with running pliers.

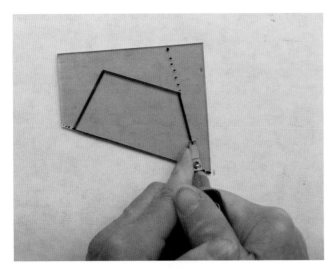

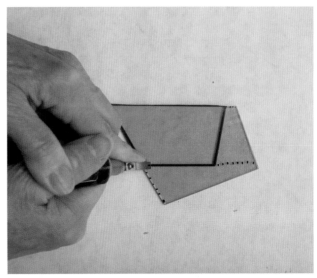

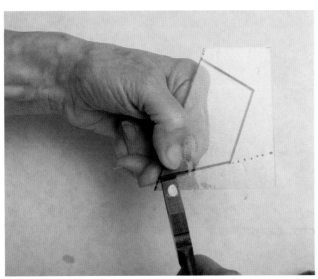

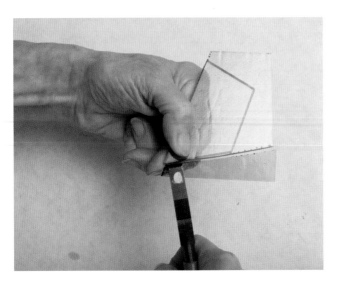

Score the final side from edge to edge. Break it off using grozing pliers.

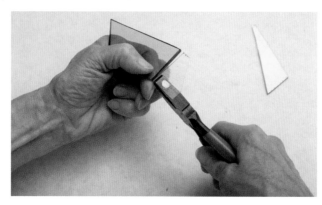

Here you can see everything that did not look like the desired shape has been taken away.

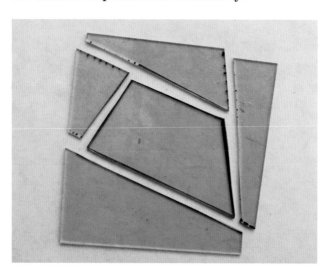

Notice that in this sample a variety of tools have been used to break the glass: hands, grozing pliers, and running pliers. This stage just gives you a feel for using these tools.

SHAPE #2

This shape has two straight parallel sides and two rounded edges.

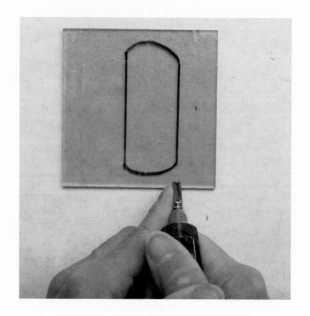

Score and break a straight side first.

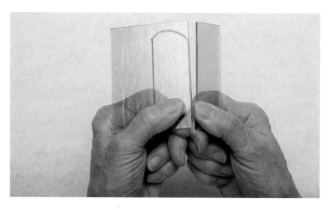

Score and break the other straight side next.

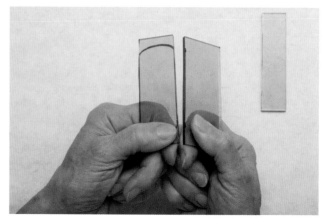

Now score an end piece, following the gentle curve with your cutter wheel. To break, angle the pliers like the curve. Notice they are placed at the edge of the score, not in the middle.

Repeat that step with the other curved end.

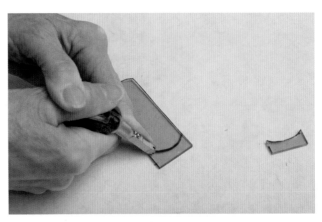

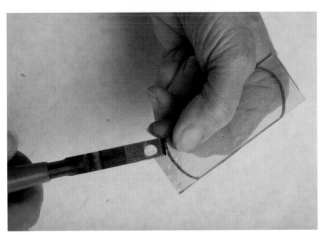

Here is the finished shape and its cut-away pieces.

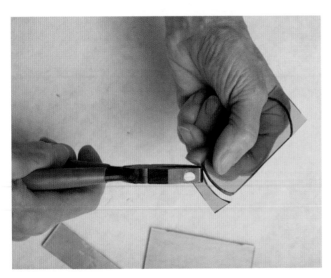

SHAPE #3

Score and break the inward curves first.

Start your score at the edge of the glass and follow the gentle curve, continuing to the opposite edge.

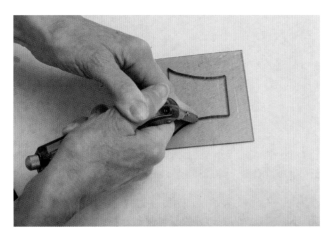

Break the score with grozing pliers, angled with the curve of the score line. The pliers should be positioned at the beginning of the score.

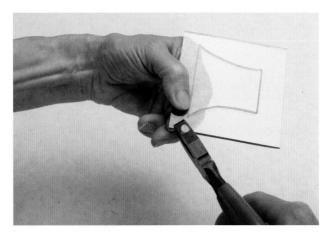

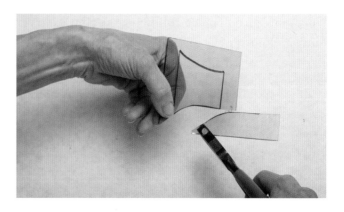

Repeat with the second gentle curve.

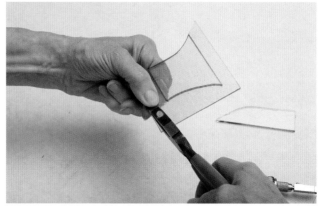

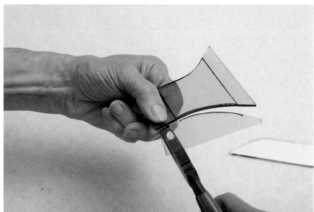

Finally, score and break off each of the straight sides.

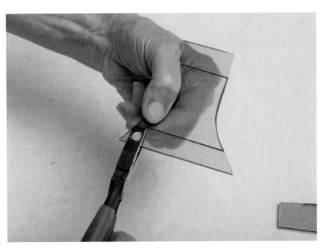

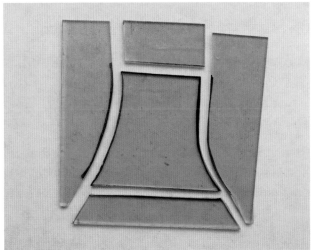

SHAPE #4

When looking at a shape like this one, the inside curve is the first side of the design to cut.

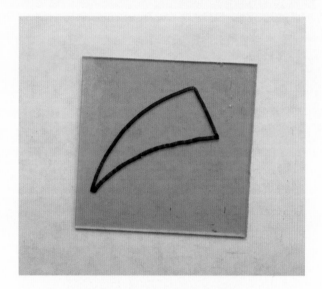

Rather than cutting this whole curve at one time, first cut across the glass just touching the edges of the shape in order to remove some excess glass.

Break off the excess.

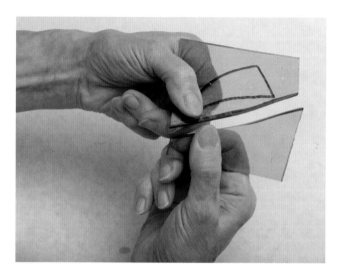

Now score the shallow curve that remains.

Break this off with grozing pliers.

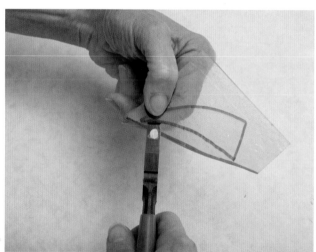

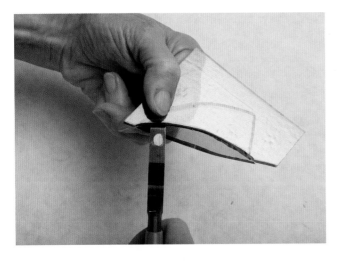 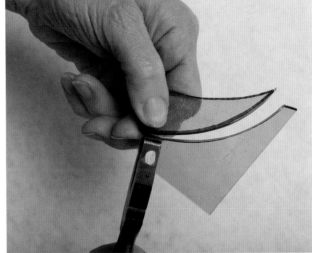

Score and then break the straight side.

 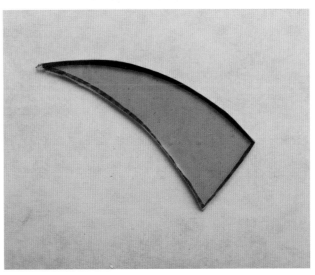

Score and break off the gentle outward curve.

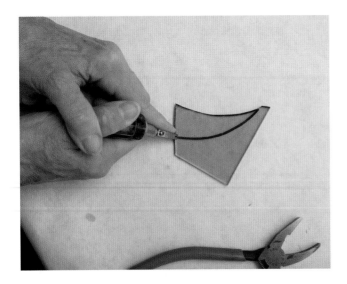

SHAPE #5

This shape has a very deep curve. In order to successfully cut a deep curve, break it down into parts.

First, draw a line across the glass, just touching the pointed ends of the shape.

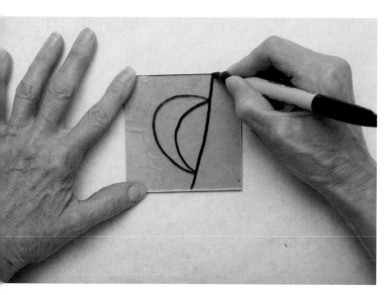

Next, draw in a gentle arc, leading from the inside curve.

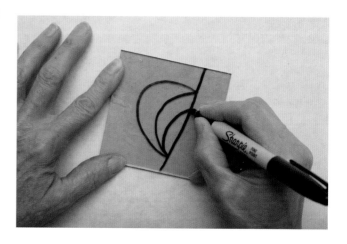

Then draw another gentle arc, coming from the opposite point of this shape.

This is the numbered order in which you will score and break these pieces.

To begin cutting this shape, score and break away the excess glass, just touching the ends of the shape.

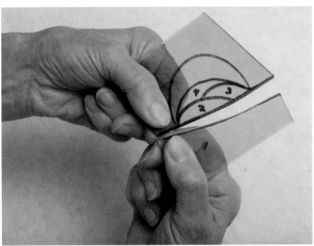

Now score the first curve.

Use grozing pliers to break off the small, curvy piece.

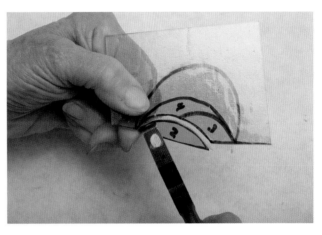

Now come in from the opposite side to score the next section.

Use grozing pliers at the end of that curve to break it off.

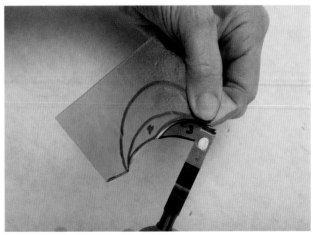

Lastly, complete the inner curve by scoring and breaking it off with grozing pliers.

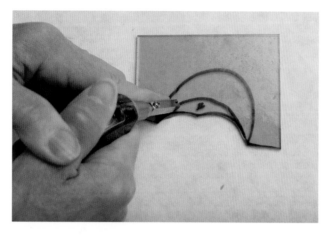

The outside of this shape is too extreme to successfully score and break in one cut, so it is done in a series of three steps.

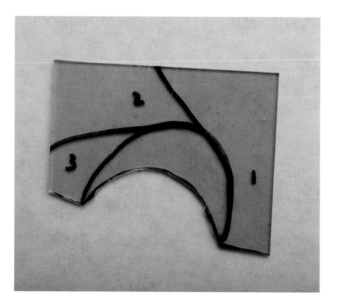

To cut the outside curve, score the arc for just a bit and continue to an outside edge. Break that section off with grozing pliers. Place them at the opposite end to break this piece. Breaking toward a point makes it more likely to be a successful break.

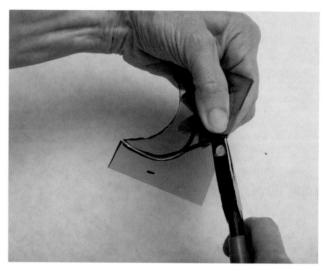

Score the next section of the curve, going to an outside edge.

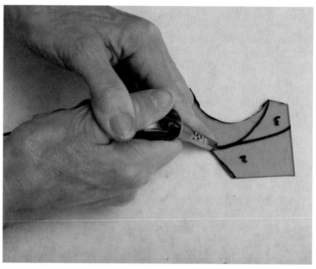

Break that off close to the start of the score.

Now break off the extra nubs.

Score and break the remaining section.

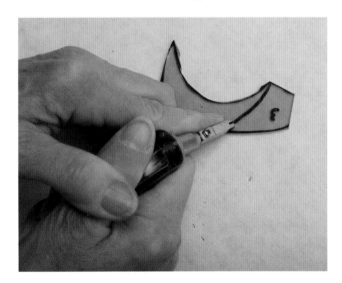

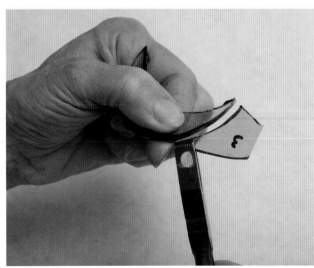

Use the grozing pliers to remove any sharp points that remain from the previous scores and breaks.

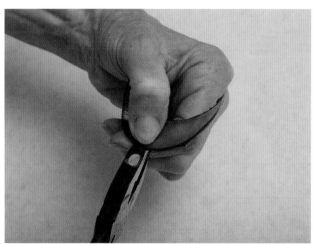

SHAPE #6

Find which side of the diamond has the deepest inner curve and begin there.

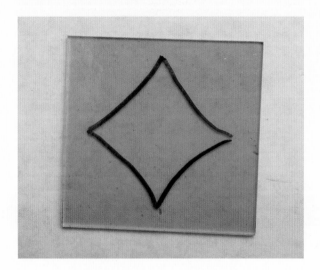

Score and break away excess glass first.

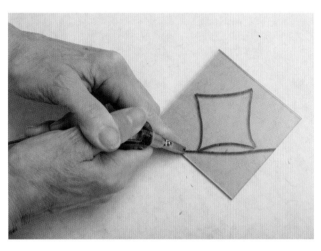

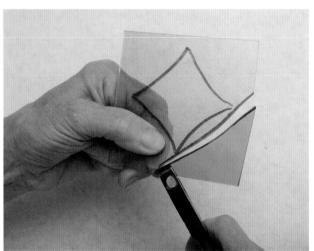

Then, score the curve and break it with grozing pliers.

The remaining curves are quite shallow, so they can be scored and broken without removing excess glass first. Score the second side and break it away.

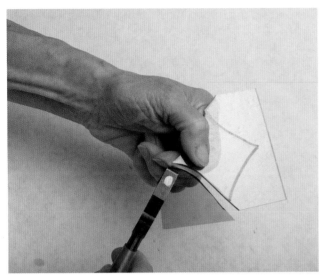

Score and break away the third side.

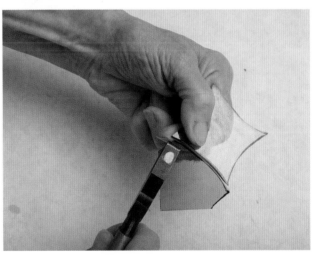

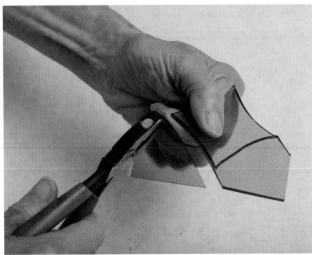

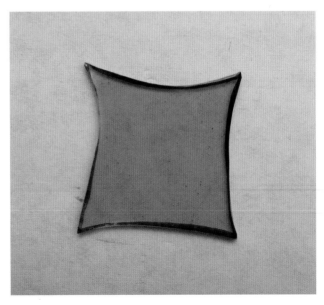

SHAPE #7

Identify which curve is deepest and cut that side first.

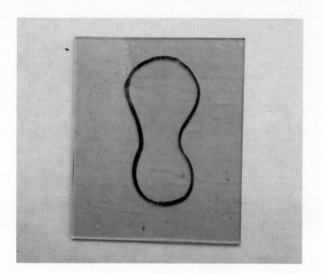

Now score the inner curve on that side and break it with grozing pliers.

Score and break away excess glass, just touching the edges of the design.

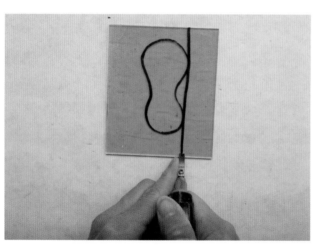

Score and break away excess glass on the other side, just touching the edges of the design.

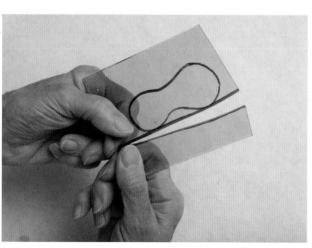

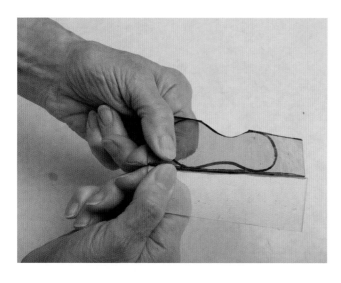

Score the inside curve and break away the glass with grozing pliers.

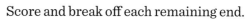

Score and break off each remaining end.

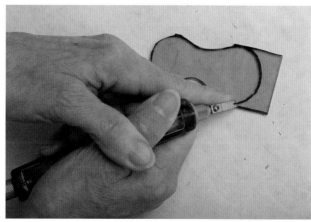

You can see in the sample that in breaking off the final end, it split in two.

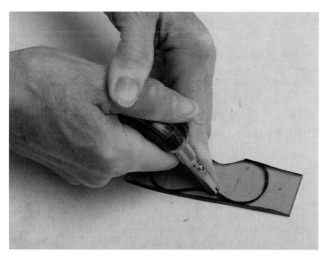

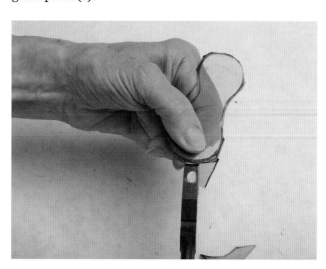

Should this happen in your practice, simply go back with the grozing pliers and remove the remaining glass piece(s).

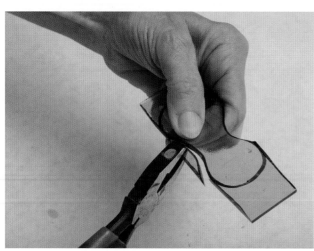

Use the grozing pliers to remove any sharp points that remain from the previous scores and breaks.

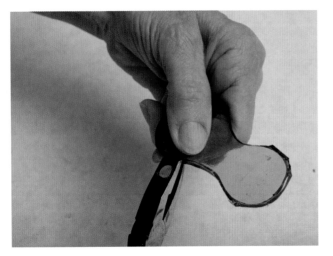

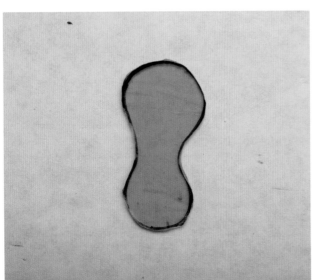

SHAPE #8

For this shape, cut the inner curve first. The glass on the outside will keep your piece more stable as you remove the deep curve.

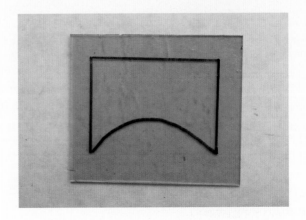

As you did with Shape #5, draw in the lines for cutting a deep curve.

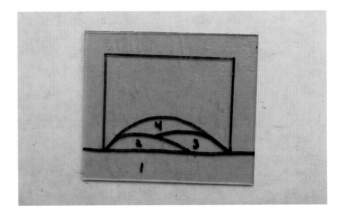

Score and break away excess glass along the bottom of the design.

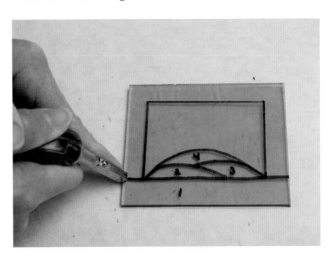

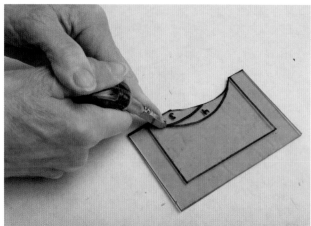
Go to the opposite side to score and break the next curve.

Score and break the first small curve.

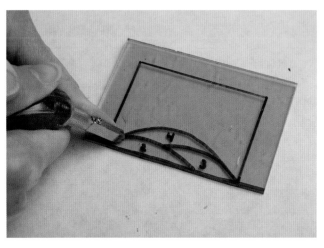

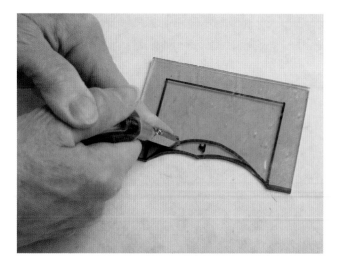
Score and break the final curve.

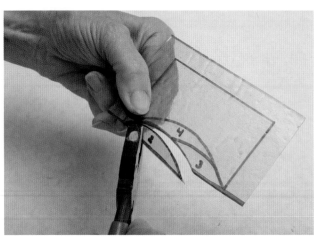

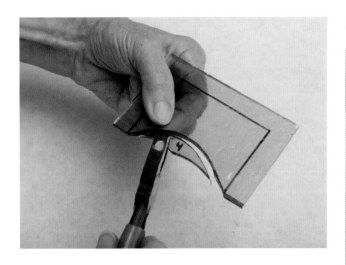

Now you can successfully score and break the straight sides.

Score the first side. Using grozing pliers, break the glass toward the pointed end.

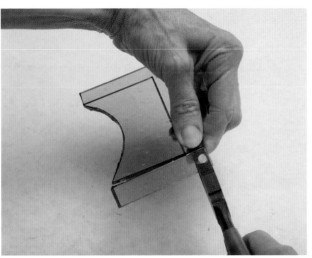

Score and break the second side.

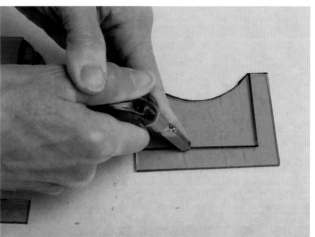

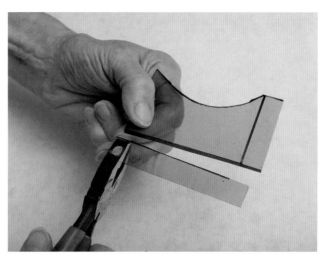

Score and break the final side, again breaking toward the pointed end.

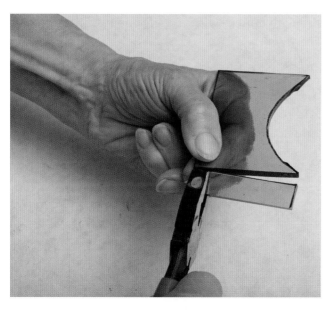

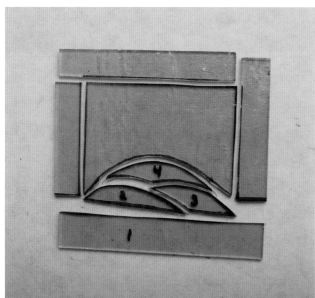

SHAPE #9

Cutting a circle out of glass is not as difficult as it may seem. If you use multiple scores and breaks, you will have a successful piece.

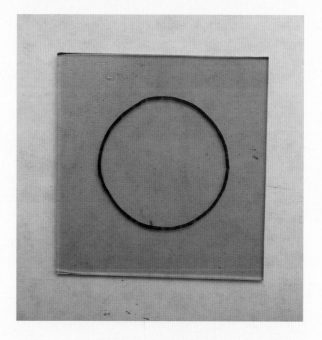

Begin by drawing in your cut lines. The first score should come in at an angle, follow part of the circle, and continue to the edge of the glass.

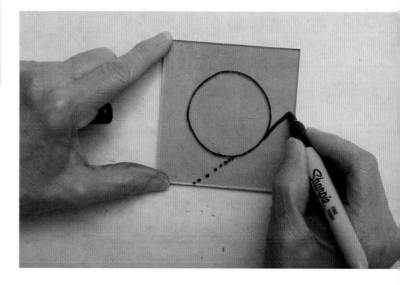

The next score should begin where your last one left off the circle, follow the arc, and continue to the edge of the glass.

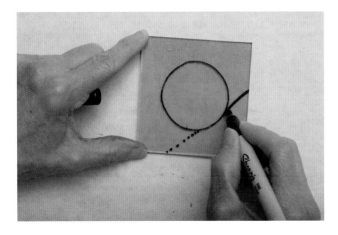

A third score should continue along the arc and go to the edge of the glass. The final section should be cut in one piece.

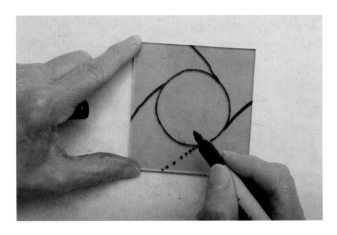

Begin your first score, following the lines you've drawn.

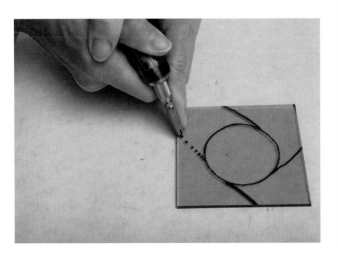

Break that piece with grozing pliers.

Score the second segment and break it off.

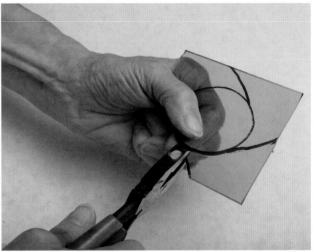

Score the third section and break it off.

Score the remaining arc and break off that piece.

Here are all the pieces cut from practice glass.

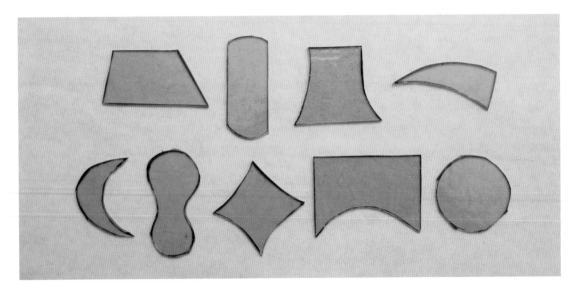

After successfully completing these practice pieces, you will be ready to tackle a stained glass project with a variety of shapes.

CUTTING GLASS WITH A PAPER PATTERN

In our classroom, we find that students are most successful in cutting glass pieces using a paper pattern that has been glued to a piece of glass. Try cutting out this sample piece following all the same principles learned in the practice session. The pattern is in chapter 13.

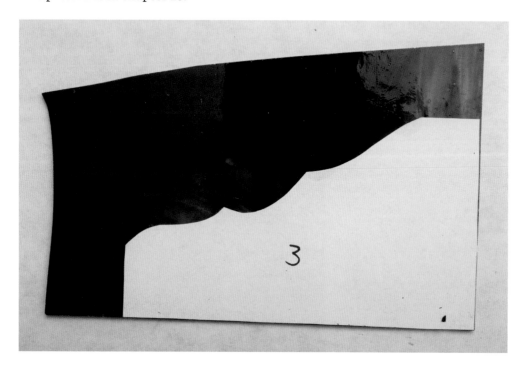

Begin by cutting the side of the design that has the inner curves. Draw in a line to get rid of excess glass first.

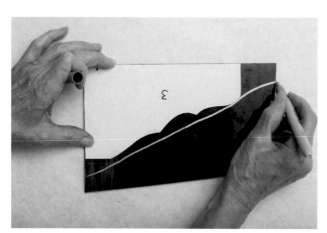

Score and break off the excess glass.

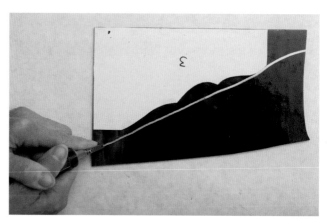

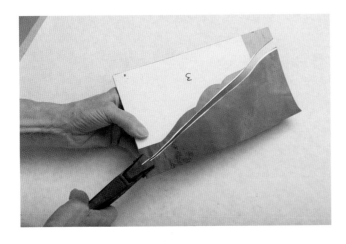

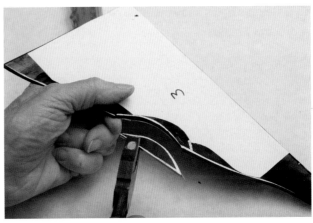

The center curve is the deepest, so cut it next. Break down this curve into two scores and breaks.

Go back and score the remaining part of this deep curve. Your cutter wheel should be as close to the edge of the paper pattern as possible.

Score the first line you have drawn and break out this piece with your grozing pliers.

Break off that piece.

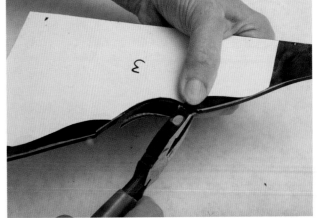

This next curve is shallow enough to do in one score and break.

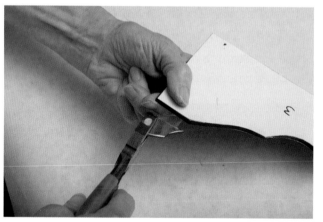

Score and break off the remaining straight sides.

Remember to break toward the point.

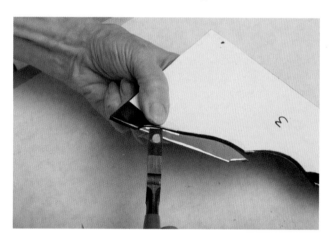

Score and break the final curve, breaking toward the point with grozing pliers.

Each score and break is right up along the edge of the paper. The more accurate your cutting is at this point the more time you will save at every subsequent step along the way.

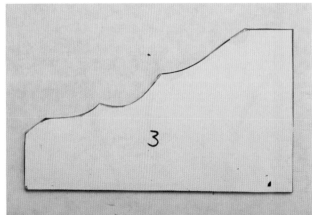

6
COPPER FOIL SUNFLOWER PANEL

IF YOU HAVE PRACTICED THE BASIC GLASS CUTTING TECHNIQUES set out in chapter 5, you are ready to put your new skills to use on your first project: a copper foil stained glass panel.

Additional skills you will learn during the construction of this panel include preparing a paper pattern, using a grinder to smooth glass edges, and applying copper foil to the glass pieces. After mastering these steps, you will move on to soldering the panel together and framing the panel with lead came. You will also learn cleaning and polishing steps that will bring a beautiful glow to your finished work.

Once you have completed the project, you can hang your stained glass panel in a window where the sun shining through it will brighten your entire room. The skills you will learn in creating your first project will improve with practice, and will open new opportunities for you in the art of stained glass!

SUPPLY LIST

- ○ Paper pack: oak tag, carbon paper, tracing paper
- ○ Pattern
- ○ Drawing tools: pencil and silver permanent marker, black permanent marker
- ○ Ruler
- ○ Masking tape
- ○ Scissors
- ○ Pattern shears for foil
- ○ Rubber cement
- Glass
  - ○ 1 square foot for the background
  - ○ 2 square feet for the flower petals
  - ○ 1 square foot for the flower center

  We used Oceanside's Sky Blue Waterglass (S5331) for the background, Oceanside's Yellow/Amber Corsica (S606181) for the flower petals, and Oceanside's Brown/Gold Streaky Granite (S41115G) for the flower center.
- ○ Safety glasses
- ○ Bench brush
- ○ Homasote board or work surface
- ○ Glass cutter
- ○ Glass cutting oil
- ○ Grozing/breaking pliers

(continued on next page)

- ○ Running pliers
- ○ Glass grinder
- ○ 7/32-inch black-backed copper foil
- ○ Fid
- ○ Craft knife
- ○ Lead came: 1 6-foot ¼-inch U channel
- ○ Lead vise
- ○ Lead cutters
- ○ Lead board with 90 degree angle corner
- ○ Horseshoe nails, approximately 1 dozen
- ○ Glazing hammer
- ○ Flux and brush
- ○ Solder
- ○ Soldering iron, stand, and wet sponge
- ○ Layout strips and pins
- ○ 30°-60°-90° tool
- ○ Needle-nose pliers
- ○ Hanging rings: 2, made of pretinned copper wire
- ○ Mild detergent
- ○ Wash basins
- ○ Newspaper
- ○ Flux and patina neutralizer
- ○ Protective gloves
- ○ Black patina for lead and solder
- ○ Small sponge
- ○ Stained glass polish
- ○ Towels

1 Begin with a paper packet that is larger than your pattern. A paper packet consists of a sheet of oak tag or heavy card stock, which will become the pattern for rebuilding your panel; a sheet of carbon paper, which will transfer the design to the oak tag when you trace your pattern; and a sheet of tracing paper, which will be cut apart and glued to the glass so you will be able to accurately cut your glass pieces.

2 It is important to arrange your paper packet in the proper order. Begin with the oak tag or heavy card stock on the bottom. Next, place the carbon paper with the carbon side down against the oak tag. The next layer will be your full-size pattern, faceup. Finally, the tracing paper becomes your top layer.

3 Even up the edges of your completed paper packet and place it on your work surface. Center your pattern within the packet, and tape the paper packet edges to your work surface.

4 Use a ruler and a pencil to trace the perimeter of your design. Press firmly so that the markings transfer well through all layers and onto the oak tag. Continue to trace over all pattern lines until your design is complete. Slight imperfections in your tracing should not affect your finished project, but any lines that vary by more than 1/4 inch should be redrawn.

5 Before taking the paper packet apart, number each piece of the design. This will prevent confusion when assembling the glass pieces for soldering. For this design, we used a left-to-right numbering system, but use whatever system seems logical to you.

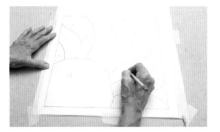

6 Next, color-code your pattern pieces. This will help identify which pattern pieces to glue on which glass color once the pattern has been cut apart. There are three colors for this project:

- Sky—Sky Blue Waterglass. These pattern pieces are designated with an S.

- Flower petals—Yellow/Amber Corsica. These pattern pieces are designated with a Y.

- Flower center—Brown/Gold Streaky Granite. These pattern pieces are designated with a B.

7 The last thing you will mark on your pattern will be directional arrows. These arrows will designate the direction in which you want the color or texture to follow. In our panel we wanted the sky to have a horizontal texture, so we drew horizontal arrows on those pattern pieces.

For the flower petals, we wanted the color and texture of the glass to ray out from the flower center, so we marked our arrows on the pattern pieces in that manner.

We wanted the texture in our brown flower center to angle toward the petals, and marked that pattern piece accordingly.

8 Remove the tape from your pattern pack and pull the pieces apart, revealing a hard copy of the pattern on the oak tag. Your original pattern will remain intact so that you can re-create the design at a later time if you wish.

9 Use the tracing paper copy of your paper pack to create the pattern to cut out the glass pieces. Set aside the rest of the paper pack for later use.

Using regular scissors, cut along the perimeter of your tracing paper pattern. Follow the pattern precisely.

10 The rest of the pattern will be cut out with a pair of pattern shears designed for copper foil projects. Pattern shears are unique in that they have a single blade on top and two blades on the bottom. These shears remove a tiny sliver of paper from each pattern piece; this allows room for the copper foil and the glass pieces to fit together nicely.

The best way to cut with pattern shears is to keep the jaws open wide and take small cuts. Center the top blade on the pattern lines.

11 After all pattern pieces are cut out, reassemble on the oak tag. You will notice a small gap between each pattern piece.

12 Place each S pattern piece on the Sky Blue Waterglass. When positioning pattern pieces on the glass, you can use the straight edges of the glass to your advantage. Allow enough space between each pattern piece to be able to separate them before cutting out individual shapes. Line up the arrows on the pattern with the direction of the texture in the water glass. Water glass has a gentle texture and is smooth enough to cut on the rippled side.

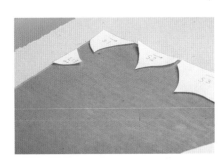

13 Turn over each pattern piece and apply rubber cement to the back of the paper, covering the piece thoroughly. Replace each pattern onto the glass, making sure the edges and points are well-adhered. Set this glass aside to allow the glue to dry.

14 Moving on to the Yellow/Amber Corsica, line up the directional arrows with the color designs in the glass. Arrange the pattern pieces so there is enough space between them to allow you to separate the pieces before cutting out their specific shapes. Glue the pattern pieces to the smooth side of the glass with rubber cement.

15 We chose a heavily textured Brown/Gold Streaky Granite glass for our flower center so as to feature that texture on the face of the panel. It would be very difficult to cut the textured side of this glass. In order to get a proper piece cut out, you will put the glue on the front of the pattern and place it facedown on the smooth side of the glass.

16 Once all the pattern pieces are glued onto the glass, allow the glue to dry for a few minutes.

1 It is time to cut out the glass, so put on your safety glasses. Your first cuts will be to separate the pieces. Break each score with your running pliers. Continue to score and break until all pieces of glass are separated.

2 Now cut out each individual shape, following the pattern as closely as possible. Remember to use the principles learned in chapter 5 to make successful scores and breaks. When using a paper pattern, the last cut on each side should be right up to the edge of the pattern.

3 Here is a rather deep curve. Remember to take an initial score to remove excess glass and expose the curve. Then, go back to precisely cut along the curve.

4 While you are cutting the remaining glass pieces, remember to sweep away any excess glass, including small chips to keep your work surface clean.

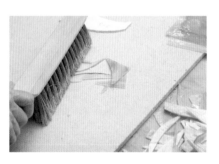

5 Lastly, cut out the brown flower center. You will recall that because this glass is heavily textured, the pattern has been turned upside down and glued to the smoother side of the glass. As you cut, break down each side into multiple scores and breaks. Cut the straight sides last.

When all the glass pieces are cut, it is time to use the grinder to smooth the glass edges. To keep the grinder bit cool, and to keep the glass chipping to a minimum, add water to the grinder according to the manufacturer's recommendations. Do not overfill, as this can damage the grinder's motor and risks causing an electrical shock. Wet the grinder's sponge and place it in the proper position. Make sure the eye shield is in place and always wear safety glasses while you operate your grinder.

3 Remove the pattern from each piece of glass and wipe the glass with a towel to dry it. Immediately write the number of the pattern piece onto the glass with a permanent marker.

1 Grind every edge of each piece of glass. You are grinding to remove any excess glass, but you are also roughing up the edge of the glass a bit. This will help the copper foil tape stick well to the glass when you reach that stage. Grind right up to the edge of your paper pattern, but not beyond. Take care not to grind off any of the glass points.

2 Set up the oak tag pattern on your work board. Pin layout strips along the left side and the bottom of the pattern to keep the edges straight. You can check the corner you have created with a 30°-60°-90° tool to make sure the corner is square.

4 Place each numbered piece of glass onto your oak tag pattern. Remember to flip the brown flower center so that it fits into your panel with the textured side up.

5 With all the glass pieces laid out, check that everything fits together well. There should be a small, even space between each piece to allow for the copper foil. Any areas that do not fit well will need some additional grinding. As you can see here, this bump needs to be ground to fit more closely with the neighboring pieces. After touch-up grinding, be sure to dry the glass again before replacing it on the pattern.

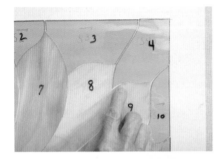

6 Add a layout strip at the top of the panel and at the right side of the panel. Pin the layout strips into place.

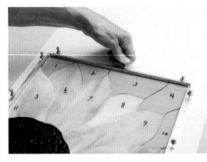

7 Check the corners with the 30°-60°-90° tool to make sure the corners are square.

8 Once the pieces all fit into place, take each one individually and wash the grinder dust off of its edges. Wash with a mild detergent, rinse, and dry. If the number washes off, make sure to write it back on the glass before proceeding.

COPPER FOILING

1 Now that everything is clean, you are ready to foil the glass. Solder will not stick to glass, so by wrapping the glass in adhesive-backed copper foil, the solder will have something to adhere to. To foil the glass, you will need a roll of copper foil, regular scissors, and a fid.

2 Peel back the protective paper from the end of the roll of foil to expose the adhesive black backing. You are using a black-backed foil to match the black patina you will later put on the project.

3 To begin the foiling process, place the glass onto the adhesive side of the foil, centering the glass so there is an even amount of foil on either side. It is best to begin the foil away from a corner. Continue turning the glass while you are pressing it against the foil. Make sure there are no gaps between the glass and the foil, especially when working with inside curves.

4 When you reach your starting point again, overlap the foil about a quarter of an inch. Make sure the sides line up well and cut off the excess foil.

Now use your thumb and forefinger to crimp the corners. Press in from one direction, then down from the other. Repeat this step with each corner.

5 Now take your thumb and forefinger and slide them up the edge, folding the foil over the glass on both sides at the same time.

6 Use a plastic fid to burnish the edges of the foil onto the glass. Use the broad edge of this tool to smooth the foil.

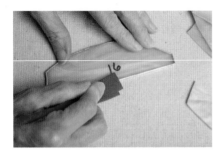

8 Smooth the foil on the edge by running the fid along the sides of the glass as well.

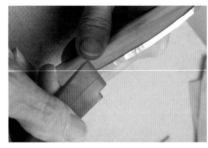

10 Once all the pieces have been foiled, lay them back onto the pattern in their proper places. They should fit snugly within the borders of the pattern.

7 Turn the glass over and repeat that process on the back. If there is a texture on the back of the glass, take extra care to make sure the foil is well-adhered.

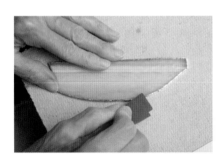

9 If the overlap on any piece is a little off center, you can use a craft knife to trim off the excess foil.

Now you are ready to solder.

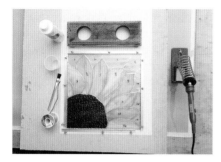

1 If you have an adjustable temperature control iron, set it at the temperature recommended for soldering copper foil seams. Our soldering iron is set to 410 degrees Celsius.

Make sure the sponge is wet in the soldering iron stand.

Pour some flux into a disposable cup so that you do not contaminate the bottle. Dip the brush into the flux and wipe it on the edge of the cup. Paint the flux over all of the copper foil seams. The purpose of flux is to clean the oxidation from the foil surface so that the solder will flow smoothly.

2 Hold the spool of solder so that about 8 inches of solder extends from the roll.

3 Put your hand over the soldering iron, the same way you would hold a flashlight.

4 Put the end of the solder where pieces of glass intersect. Come down flat with the soldering iron to melt about a quarter of an inch of solder onto the copper foil seam. Lift the solder up first, then lift the iron. This will melt a tack of solder to hold the glass pieces together. Continue to tack every place where corners of glass intersect and then add a tack of solder at each of the seams near the edges of the panel.

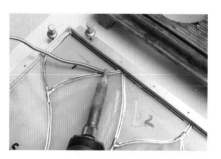

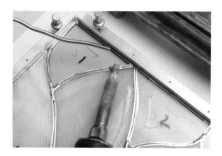

5 After each junction has been tack soldered, remove the pins and layout strips. Pull the pattern out from underneath the panel. Now you can move the panel in any direction so that you can comfortably solder each seam.

6 Again, begin with about 8 inches of solder extended from the spool. Take your iron out of the holder and wipe each side of the tip on the wet sponge to clean it.

7 Place the tip of the soldering iron on its edge and set it against the copper foil. Tilt the iron back about a quarter of a turn and place the end of the solder onto the flat side of the iron tip.

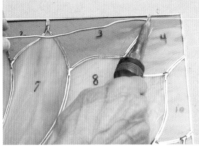

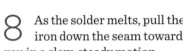

8 As the solder melts, pull the iron down the seam toward you in a slow, steady motion.

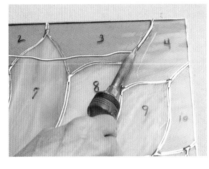

9 As the solder melts away, unspool more so that you always have 6 to 8 inches of solder extended and you are holding only the spool. Heat will flow up the length of solder, so make sure your fingers are back from the unspooled amount. Continue soldering slowly, one seam at a time. We find that many of our students tend to solder too quickly at first. If you find that you are not getting adequate coverage with your solder, slow down!

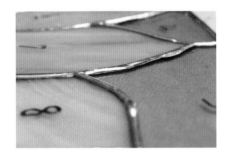

10 The first coat of solder does not look even or consistent. There are many spots that are flat and others that are a bit bumpy. This is typical and will smooth out with an additional layer of solder.

11 After the first coat of solder is complete, paint a second coat of flux over each solder seam.

12 For the second coat, you will again place the iron on the seam, starting straight up and then turning it back a quarter turn to reveal the flat edge. Place the end of the solder against the flat side of the iron. Slowly pull your iron down the seam, allowing the second coat to melt into the first.

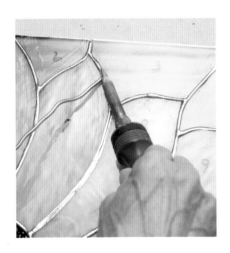

You can see the difference between one coat of solder and two.

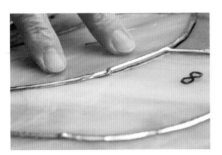

13 Continue adding a second layer of solder to each seam of the panel. Smooth any rough spots by slowly pulling your iron over the seam once more. After all seams are soldered, let the panel cool for about 30 seconds.

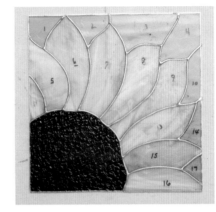

14 Carefully turn the panel over. On the back you will notice that some of the solder has come through from the front and has filled in any gaps between pieces.

15 Paint the foil lines with flux. Then proceed with soldering the back of the panel. You do not need to "tack solder" this side, because the piece is already held together. On the back side you may only need one coat of solder to get the same beaded look that you got from two coats on the front. In some areas you may need to add a second layer of solder if the seam appears flat. Add whatever combination of one to two layers of solder so that the back of the panel looks as nice as the front.

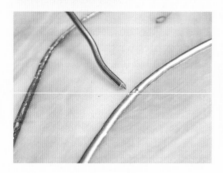
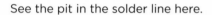

See the pit in the solder line here.

Sometimes flux gets caught in the solder and boils up to the surface. To fix that area, just put the side of the iron down onto the solder until it melts, then lift the iron straight up again.

16 When the back is completely soldered, carefully turn the panel over so the front side faces up. You may discover an area where solder has melted through from the opposite side of the panel.

In order to fix it, add some flux, then place the side of the iron over the bump until the solder melts. Lift the iron straight up.

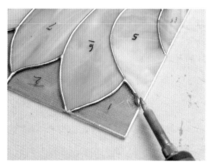

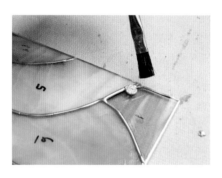

1 For the frame, use 1/4-inch U-channel lead. Stretch the 6-foot length of lead with a lead vise. To stretch it, put the end of the lead, channel side up, into the vise and clamp it down. Hold the other end with pliers and pull the lead straight until you feel it give just a bit. Stretching the lead makes it stronger and straighter, creating more stability for the longevity of the panel.

2 Cut the lead into manageable pieces to make it easier to frame the panel. Since this panel is 12" square, cut four pieces of lead that are about 14 inches long.

3 Cut a sample piece of lead that is just a couple inches long. With this sample piece, test the edges of the panel to see if the lead will fit over the solder seams.

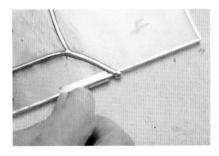

At any place it does not fit, take the iron and remove about a quarter inch of solder from the panel by melting it off the edge.

4 Turn the panel over and do the same for each seam on the back. Then stand the panel up on end and use the iron to clean the excess solder off the edges of the panel. Use the sample piece of lead again to test that it fits over every seam of the panel.

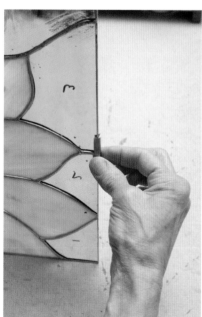

5 Transfer the panel to a lead board, made from 1/2-inch plywood with a 90 degree angle permanently attached— this one is made with two pieces of 1/2 x 3/4-inch wood strips.

6 You will need to begin framing with a good edge on the lead. Use lead cutters to cut a nice, straight edge to work with on the first strip of lead.

7 The side pieces of lead will go fully from top to bottom, and the top and bottom pieces will fit in between. Lay the left lead strip in place, extending to the bottom of the lead board.

PRO TIP

To cut lead properly, always use your lead cutters perpendicular to the open channel of the lead strip. The flat side of the cutters will leave a clean, straight cut.

8 Lay the bottom piece of lead into place, butting up against the left one.

9 Insert the panel into the U-channel lead.

10 Take the sample piece of lead and lay it in position on the right side of the panel. Scratch the bottom piece of lead with a nail to mark where you will cut it.

11 Take the lead off the board and cut it at your mark. Place the bottom piece of lead back into position and insert the panel back in the U-channel lead.

12 Lay the top lead into place, butting up against the left one. Use the sample piece of lead on the right side to mark the top piece where you will cut it.

13 Cut the lead at the mark. Place the top lead back into its place.

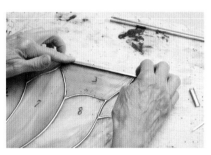

14 Use horseshoe nails to hold the top lead snugly against the panel. Hammer the horseshoe nails into the board.

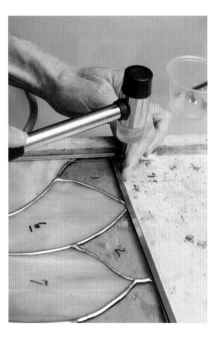

15 Lay the right lead into place and secure it with horseshoe nails. The left and right lead pieces will extend beyond the top of the panel at this time. You will cut those off later.

16 Lead framing is very soft. If you have a temperature control iron, turn your iron down to 360 degrees Celsius. If your iron does not have a temperature control, you will need to use a separate rheostat or cool the iron on a wet sponge. An iron that is too hot will melt through the lead framing.

17 Add a bit of flux to each corner of the frame, as well as to the ends of each seam where they meet the lead came.

18 Put a dot of solder onto the iron tip.

19 Bring the dot of solder down onto the corner of the lead framing where two pieces intersect.

20 Bring the iron straight up as soon as it attaches.

21 Add a dot of solder to each of the remaining three corners.

22 You will also connect each solder seam to the lead frame. Put a dot of solder on the end of the iron. Melt that solder dot into the end of the seam, then rock the iron back to attach the seam to the lead frame. Lift the iron up as soon as it attaches. Do not linger on the lead, as it will melt more quickly than the seams of solder.

Note: Do not spread the solder up and down the lead framing. It will just get bumpy and will never fully smooth out the way a solder seam does in the panel. This part of the project is not as forgiving.

23 Once the seams are all connected to the frame, remove the nails and move your panel back to the Homasote board.

24 Turn the panel over so that you can solder the back seams.

25 Flux each corner of the frame and the connection points for each seam.

26 Proceed as you did on the front, connecting each seam to the frame and also adding a dot of solder over the junction of the framing at the corners.

27 Now stand the panel up and trim off the lead that extends beyond the top of the frame.

28 The holes that remain from trimming the lead can be filled in with solder.

29 Flux the area of the hole and add just a dot or two of solder with your iron to fill the space. You can also fill the holes on the bottom of the frame.

Don't forget to recycle your lead scraps!

30 Flux the two rings that will become the hooks. Also flux the two corners that will be the top, back side of the panel.

31 Hold one of the rings with a pair of pliers. Position the split in the ring over the corner of the panel's frame.

32 With a dot of solder, add the ring to the corner of the panel. Add the second ring to the other corner in the same manner, soldering over the split in the ring.

1 Wash the panel with a mild detergent and water. Scrub off all the numbers and flux residue, as well as any loose solder balls. Make sure you wash both sides of the panel.

2 Rinse and dry the panel.

3 Set up some newspaper to protect your work surface and place your panel over the newspaper. Spray the panel liberally with a flux and patina neutralizer. Wipe that side dry. Turn the panel over and repeat this on the back side.

4 Silver solder lines tend to draw your eye, so add a black patina to the piece. This allows the colors of the glass to be the central focus of the panel.

5 Put on a pair of protective gloves. Shake up the black patina. Add a bit of patina to a small sponge and apply it to all of the solder lines and the lead frame. Make sure to get the edges of the frame as well as the hooks. Turn the panel over and repeat the same on the back.

6 Wash the panel gently with detergent so as not to scratch off any of the patina. Rinse the panel in cool water, which will help set the patina. Dry the panel with a towel.

7 Again, spray the panel with the flux and patina neutralizer and dry it. Turn the panel over and repeat this step on the back.

8 Drizzle glass polish onto one side and rub it around with a clean towel.

9 Spread the polish onto the glass, the solder lines, and the frame. Turn the panel over and do the same to the back surface. Let the polish film up for a few minutes on both sides of the panel.

10 Take a clean area of the towel and buff each side of the panel to a clean, beautiful shine.

11 Your panel is now ready to hang in a sunny window!

7

LEAD CAME
TRADITIONAL PANEL

NOW THAT YOU HAVE COMPLETED THE COPPER FOIL PANEL, you may enjoy using those skills and adding new ones to create this lead came project.

You will learn to use lead came between the pieces of glass instead of applying the copper foil tape. The came will be soldered at each intersection rather than using long seams of solder. Once the lead has been soldered together at the joints, you will apply a glazing compound to seal the glass in place.

The lead came process was developed hundreds of years ago and is the technique used to create the beautiful stained glass windows in cathedrals and churches.

We have chosen a traditional design to showcase this age-honored technique.

- ○ Paper pack: oak tag, carbon paper, tracing paper
- ○ Pattern
- ○ Drawing tools: pencil, silver permanent marker, and black permanent marker
- ○ Ruler
- ○ Masking tape
- ○ Scissors
- ○ Pattern shears for lead
- ○ Rubber cement

  Glass
  - ○ 1 square foot for the background
  - ○ ½ square foot for the border
  - ○ Small pieces of two complementary colors

  We used Wissmach's Clear Seedy (01S) for the background, Wissmach's Pale Purple Ripple (418RIP) for the border, and Wissmach's English Muffle Texture of Dark Purple (4924) and Light Olive (4915) for the design portions.

- ○ Safety glasses
- ○ Bench brush
- ○ Homasote board or work surface
- ○ Glass cutter
- ○ Glass cutting oil
- ○ Grozing/breaking pliers
- ○ Running pliers
- ○ Glass grinder

(continued on next page)

- ◯ Mild detergent

- ◯ Wash basins

- ◯ Fid

- ◯ Towels

- ◯ Lead came: 1 6-foot-length ¼-inch round U-channel lead; 2 6-foot-length ³⁄₁₆-inch flat H-channel lead; 1 6-foot-length ⅛-inch round (or flat) H-channel lead

- ◯ Lead vise

- ◯ Lead cutters

- ◯ Lead board with 90 degree angle corner

- ◯ Horseshoe nails, 1 to 2 dozen

- ◯ Glazing hammer

- ◯ Tweezers

- ◯ Flux and brush

- ◯ Solder

- ◯ Soldering iron, stand and wet sponge

- ◯ Wire cutters

- ◯ 6 inches 14-gauge pretinned copper wire Newspaper

- ◯ Glazing cement

- ◯ Safety mask

- ◯ Whiting

- ◯ 2 brushes for cement and whiting

- ◯ Steel wool

- ◯ Plexiglass for mixing cement

- ◯ Putty knife

- ◯ Screwdriver

- ◯ Apron

- ◯ Wooden skewer

1 Begin with a full-size pattern. Layer the paper pack as you did for the Copper Foil Panel in chapter 6. The oak tag is on the bottom, carbon paper is next, then your full-size pattern, and finally the tracing paper on top.

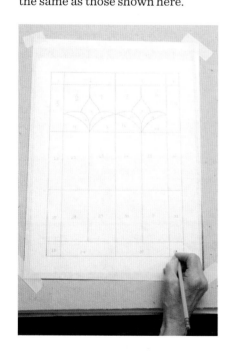

2 Trace off your pattern in the same manner as the Copper Foil Panel. Number each piece. Note that for this panel you will be building it piece by piece. Therefore, it will be easiest to follow along if your pattern pieces are numbered the same as those shown here.

3 Add color-coding letters and the directional arrows.

4 Cut the perimeter of your tracing paper pattern with regular scissors.

5 Cut out the pattern with the lead shears.

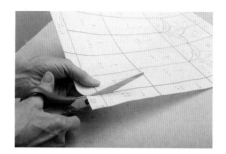

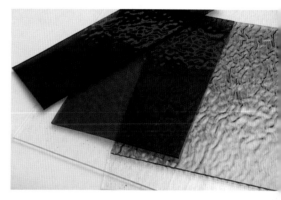

Here's the glass for this project.

PRO TIP

These are lead pattern shears. This brand of shears comes with two blades, one for foil and one for lead.

Note the difference between the amounts of paper that lead shears remove compared to foil shears. In this photo, the left snip was made by the lead shears, and the right snip was made by foil shears. Using lead shears for cutting the pattern will allow an appropriate amount of space for the lead channel between the pieces of glass in the panel.

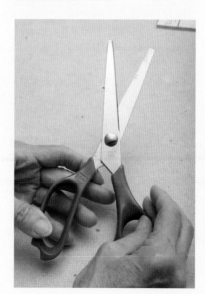

6 Glue the paper pattern to the glass, following the directional arrows.

7 Cut out each piece of glass, using the skills learned in chapter 5.

8 Grind the edges of each piece of glass, up to the edge of the paper pattern, but not beyond. Refer to the "Grinding" section of chapter 6 for proper grinding technique, if necessary.

9 Wash the glass with a mild detergent and water, rinse, dry, and number each piece with permanent marker. Here are the glass pieces ready for construction.

10 Using regular scissors, cut the oak tag pattern precisely on the bottom line of the pattern.

11 Then, cut the oak tag paper on the left line of the pattern.

12 Collect all the lead strips you will use for the project: 1/4-inch round U-channel lead for the frame, 3/16-inch flat H-channel lead for the interior, and 1/8-inch round H-channel lead for shaping around the flower designs. Note the difference between H-channel and U-channel lead.

13 Stretch the lead using a lead vise attached to a sturdy table. Place the end of the lead strip, channel side up, into the vise and clamp it down. Use a pair of pliers to hold the other end of the lead, and pull until you feel the lead stretch. This strengthens and straightens the lead strips.

14 Stretch all the strips of lead needed for the project.

15 To properly cut U-channel lead, always cut with the open channel facing up. The flat side of the pliers should be perpendicular to the open channel.

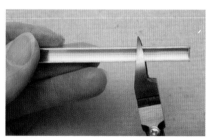

Notice the flat side of the lead cutters leaves a clean, 90 degree cut on the lead, while the angled side of the lead cutters leaves the right side of the lead crimped.

Wrong Way: Using lead cutters to cut the sides of the lead channel squashes the channel together, not allowing the glass to fit in.

Note the incorrect cut on the left piece of lead, and the appropriate cut on the right piece of lead in this photo.

When cutting H-channel lead, one of the channels should also face up.

16 Each and every piece of lead that will go into your panel needs to have a clean edge. As you build your panel, be sure to remember to cut off the angled end of the lead each time you add a new piece.

17 Cut U-channel lead into manageable lengths to work with. Since this panel is 10 x 14 inches, cut the U-channel into two 12-inch lengths and two 16-inch lengths.

18 Cut the H-channel lead in half. The 36-inch pieces will be more manageable to work with.

19 Cut about a dozen scraps of each type of lead to use as spacers throughout the building of the panel.

20 Place the oak tag pattern onto the lead board so that the bottom left corner of the pattern lines up with the 90 degree angle on the lead board.

21 Place one of the 16-inch lengths of U-channel lead along the left side, fully to the bottom of your lead board. This lead will extend a few inches beyond the top of the pattern.

22 Place one of the 12-inch lengths of U-channel lead along the bottom, starting inside the vertical channel of the lead. This lead will extend beyond the end of the panel at the right side for now.

23 To check your spacing, put one of the bottom pieces of glass in place, making sure you can still see the pattern line above it.

24 Put one of the side pieces of glass in place, again checking to see that you can still see the pattern line. If the pattern line is not visible, adjust the pattern until it is.

25 With those pieces in place, tape the pattern to the lead board on the top and on the right side.

26 Tap a nail to hold the ends of each lead strip into place beyond the end of the pattern. Pierce the lead with the nail so it cannot move as you are working.

27 Begin with the bottom left corner, putting glass piece number 33 in place.

28 Hold a scrap of H-channel lead to keep piece 33 in place. Measure the piece of lead that will be going to the right of piece number 33. While holding it in place, use a nail to scratch a mark into the lead where the inside edge of the other came meets it to form a right angle.

29 Cut the lead came at the scratch mark, making sure the channel faces up. Place the cut piece of lead into the panel to hold the corner piece of glass in place. Using the scrap of lead above the glass, tap a nail into the board to hold that scrap and secure the right H-channel lead in place.

30 Slide glass piece number 34 into position.

31 Put another small scrap of lead on the top border to hold the glass and lead in place so that you can mark where you will cut the piece of lead for the right side of glass piece 34.

32 Cut the piece of marked lead so that you have a clean edge on both sides of this lead piece.

33 Put this piece of lead into place and use a scrap piece of lead to hold it in position.

34 Slide glass piece number 35 into position. Readjust the scrap and nail it into place. Measure a piece of H-channel for between pieces 35 and 36.

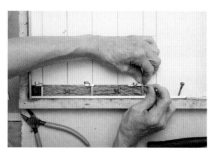

35 Use a piece of U-channel to hold number 36 into place as a spacer. Mark the bottom piece of lead using the U-channel spacer on the side as a guide to where the bottom border piece will be cut.

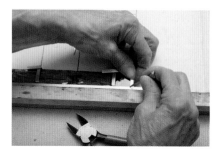

36 Pull out the nails and pieces of glass to remove the bottom border piece of lead. Cut precisely at your mark.

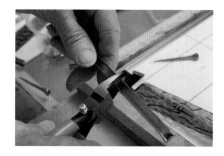

37 Place the lower border lead back into place and replace each of the pieces of glass with the lead pieces separating them.

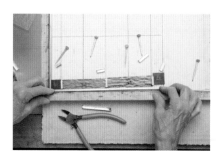

38 Nail the U-channel spacer into place at the right edge to hold the bottom row of the panel together.

39 Place one length of H-channel lead across the width of the panel. Mark it to size with a nail, using the scrap of U-channel on the edge as a guide.

40 Begin building the second row of the panel with piece 27. Use a spacer of H-channel lead to mark the height of the lead strip between glass pieces 27 and 28.

41 Continue across the second row adding each glass piece and each lead strip.

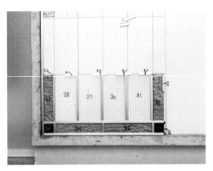

42 Place the next horizontal strip of H-channel across the tops of pieces 27 to 32.

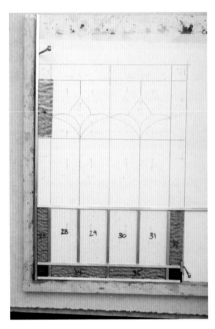

43 Nail the strip of lead into place.

44 Use a scrap of U-channel lead to mark the length of the horizontal strip.

45 Trim the lead to your mark.

46 Lay out the third row of glass pieces in the same manner.

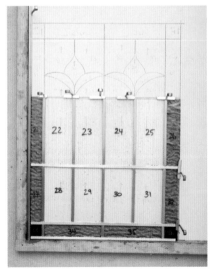

47 Again, place a horizontal strip of H-channel lead across the top of the third row of glass, mark it with a U-channel scrap to determine its length, cut it, and nail it into place.

48 Begin building the next row, putting glass piece 5 into place and cutting H-channel lead for its right border.

49 In the design portion of this panel, build each boxed section piece by piece. Use 1/8-inch H-channel lead for the smaller design portion. This lead is more pliable and easier to work with when shaping around small, curved pieces.

50 Take a scrap of 3/16-inch H-channel lead to mark where the 1/8-inch H channel needs to be cut. Note that this cut will be made at a slight angle.

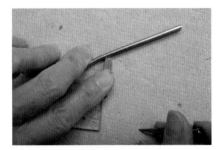

51 Here you can see the 1/8-inch lead cut around piece 11.

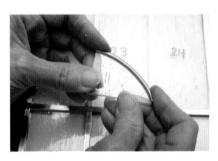

52 Place piece 11 into position.

53 Add the strip of 1/8-inch lead that you have cut.

54 Wrap a piece of 1/8-inch lead around the top of piece 12 and cut it to length.

55 Place piece 12 and its lead into position. Add piece 6 above piece 12, and use a scrap of 3/16-inch H-channel lead to hold it in place.

56 Next, place piece 15 into position. Use a scrap of 3/16-inch lead to determine where the right side of the 1/8-inch lead will be cut. Set the glass in position and add this lead.

57 Place piece 14 into position and bend the lead to follow its curve.

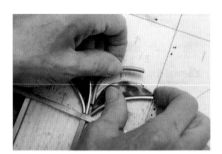

58 Place a 1/8-inch H-channel along the right side of piece 6. You can use the edge of a fid to help the lead conform to the curvature of the glass.

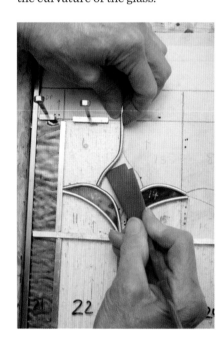

59 You may need to shift pieces 14 and 15 out of place to add piece 13.

60 With everything back into place, add a piece of 1/8-inch lead to the right side of piece 13.

61 Add piece 7 and nail it into place with a scrap of 3/16-inch H-channel lead from above.

62 Put a 3/16-inch H-channel lead on the right side of the flower box.

63 Mark this lead piece and trim it to the proper height.

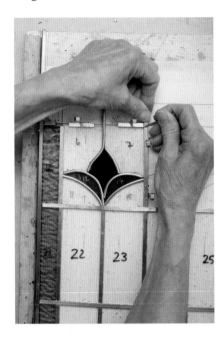

64 Build the second flower box the same as the first.

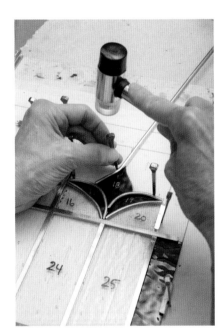

65 The right-side border of the flower box should also be 3/16-inch H-channel lead. Add border piece number 10 and nail scraps of spacer lead along the right side.

66 Cut a piece of 3/16-inch H-channel lead going from the left border to the right border across the tops of the flower boxes. Cut its length using a scrap of the 1/4-inch U-channel lead to get the appropriate width.

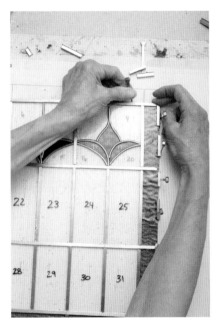

67 Nail the strip of lead into place.

68 Continue with the last row of border pieces.

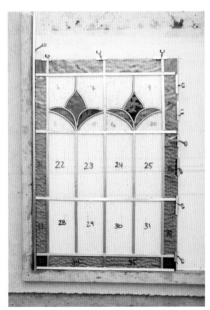

69 Cut a clean edge on the 1/4-inch U-channel lead for the top border piece, which will butt up against the left border. Mark the lead with a nail so that the cut will leave the top lead piece fitting inside both the left and right borders.

70 Nail the top border piece into place.

71 Remove the scrap pieces from the right side of the panel. With a clean cut on the bottom end of the 1/4-inch U-channel lead, fit the right frame piece into place. Tap nails into the board to keep the frame in place.

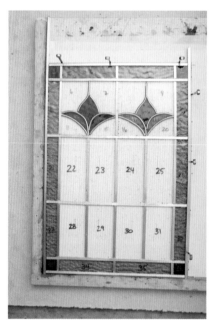

72 Review all lead joints in your panel. If there is a gap anywhere that is much more than 1/16 inch, it can be filled in with lead prior to soldering.

73 Cut a small snip of lead. Cut off the bottom flange from the H channel. Use tweezers to put the small snip of lead into the gap between lead pieces.

Don't forget to recycle your lead scraps!

74 Your panel is now ready to solder.

75 Pour some flux into a small cup to avoid contaminating the flux container.

76 Paint the flux onto every corner and every seam where lead comes together to form a joint.

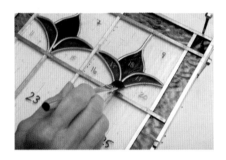

77 If you have a temperature-control iron, set the temperature to 360 degrees Celsius.

An iron without a temperature control should be used with a separate iron controller that can lower the iron's temperature.

78 Hold your iron like a flashlight.

79 Put a little bit of solder onto the flat side of the iron. Place it onto the corner joint and then lift straight up.

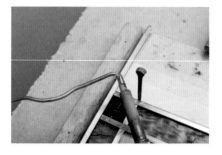

Note: Do not attempt to spread the solder around on the surface of the lead. It will not flow smoothly like it does on a copper foil seam, but will mar the lead and be stuck there forever.

80 Work systematically so as not to miss any joints, whether that is top to bottom or left to right; choose a method that works for you.

81 After each seam has been soldered, carefully turn the panel over.

82 Flux each corner and joint on the back of the panel.

83 Solder the back of the panel in the same manner as the front.

84 Trim the lead frame at the top so that the ends are flush.

85 Make two hooks by using 14-gauge pretinned copper wire, straightening it and cutting it with wire cutters into two 3-inch pieces.

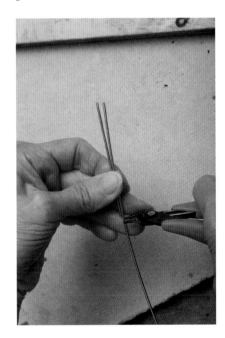

86 To make the hook, bend each piece over a pencil with an even amount of wire going down either side of the panel.

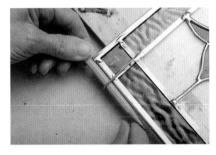

87 Leave the pencil in place as a spacer. Gently squeeze the wire with some pliers so it is flush along a lead seam.

88 Flux the wire.

89 Melt a bit of solder onto the iron and run the solder down each side of the wire to attach it to the lead.

90 Repeat with the second hook.

91 Remove the pencil. Turn over the panel.

92 Flux and solder the back of the hooks into place.

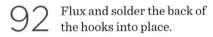

93 Fill in the holes on the ends of the panel, adding flux and then a drop or two of solder.

Note: You will notice that some of the stained glass pieces move a little within their lead channels. This is normal, but the panel needs to be cemented to make it more durable.

94 For the cement and whiting stage, make sure you wear an apron and a safety mask, and work in a well-ventilated area.

95 Open the container of cement, and if the linseed oil has separated, pour it into a small container and set it aside for later use.

96 Use a screwdriver to dig out about half of the cement from a 1-pound jar onto a scrap piece of plexiglass or other smooth, impermeable surface.

97 Use a putty knife to cut through all the clumps of cement until they are roughly the size of crumbs.

98 Pour a small amount of the reserved linseed oil onto the putty and mix it in.

99 Turn over the putty to fully mix the linseed oil into the cement until it is a smooth consistency throughout, much like a thick cake batter.

100 Scoop up a small amount of the putty with a small brush and start working it into the lead from all directions. The goal is to fill in the small space between the channels of lead and each piece of glass.

101 Continue until all channels have been filled.

102 Make sure you are wearing your safety mask for the whiting process.

103 Scoop out a small cup of whiting and sprinkle liberally on the surface of the panel.

104 Take a clean brush and work the whiting into the panel in a circular motion.

105 Once you see that the whiting has turned gray, brush it off the surface and add additional whiting to absorb the rest of the cement. Notice that the lead darkens as the whiting is brushed on, giving the panel a natural, dark patina.

106 Brush excess whiting off the panel.

107 Stand the panel up and brush some of the whiting onto the edges of the frame so that they are cleaned and darkened as well.

108 Set the panel aside and clean the work area before turning over the panel.

109 On the back of the panel, use your cement brush to work cement into the lead channels. Fully fill each channel.

110 Brush off the excess cement.

111 Sprinkle a liberal amount of whiting onto the panel.

112 Use the whiting brush to rub the whiting into the cement, cleaning the panel and darkening the lead.

113 Once again, the whiting absorbs the cement and turns gray.

114 Brush away excess whiting.

115 Wipe off any remaining whiting dust with a dry towel.

117 Let the panel sit for 24 hours.

118 Take a wooden skewer around the edges of each piece of glass, removing any excess cement. Keep the skewer vertical, not angling so that cement does not get removed from the lead channel.

116 Reclaim the unused cement and put it back in the container. Pour in any unused linseed oil for next time. Cap tightly for future use.

119 Brush off the cement debris.

120 Turn over the panel and repeat the skewering process to remove excess cement on the other side. Brush away the debris.

121 The panel is now finished. Let the finished panel sit for about a week for the cement to fully cure before hanging it up. Do not wash, patina, or polish this panel. The whiting does all of these steps simultaneously.

8
BUTTERFLY GARDEN STAKES

NOW THAT YOU HAVE COMPLETED THE COPPER FOIL PANEL AND THE LEAD CAME PANEL, YOU MAY WANT TO TRY THESE WHIMSICAL GARDEN STAKES.

Directions for using both the copper foil and the lead methods are included. Try each type of construction and discover which method you prefer.

Once you have tried your hand at these smaller projects, it will open up a world of sun catchers and small garden art pieces for you. There are many patterns and designs that will lend themselves to either method of construction. Add a hook to hang pieces in your windows or attach a brass rod for garden art.

The possibilities are endless!

COPPER FOIL BUTTERFLY GARDEN STAKE

SUPPLY LIST

- ○ Paper pattern

- ○ Permanent marker

- ○ Scissors

- ○ Rubber cement

  Glass

  - ○ Approximately ½ square foot, or 6x12-inch sheet of glass

  We used Kokomo's Yellow/White (166).

- ○ Safety glasses

- ○ Bench brush

- ○ Homasote board or work surface

- ○ Glass cutter

- ○ Glass cutting oil

- ○ Grozing/breaking pliers

- ○ Running pliers

- ○ Glass grinder

- ○ 36 inches ¼-inch silver-backed copper foil

- ○ Fid

- ○ Vise

- ○ Flux and brush

- ○ Small cup for flux

(continued on next page)

- Solder

- Soldering iron, stand, and wet sponge

- 6–inch layout strip and pins

- 2 Handy Wedges

- Needle-nosed pliers

- Wire cutters

- 36 inches 20-gauge pretinned copper wire

- Wire twister tool

- 1/8-inch brass rod, 36-inches tall

- Mild detergent

- Wash basins

- Flux and patina neutralizer

- Stained glass polish

- Towels

1 Using regular scissors, cut out the perimeter of the pattern and cut apart the wing sections. Because this is more of a free-form project, there is no need to use pattern shears to cut out the pattern.

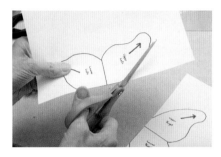

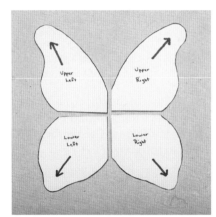

2 Place each pattern piece on the glass, lining up the directional arrows with the color grain or pattern in the glass. Make sure there is space between each pattern piece to separate the glass pieces.

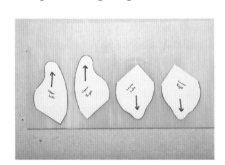

3 Brush rubber cement onto the back of each pattern piece and glue them all into place on the glass.

4 Using your glass cutter, score the glass between the pattern pieces and use running pliers to break the glass, separating each piece from the others.

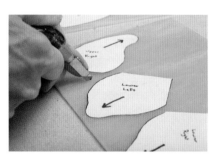

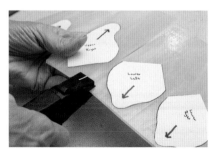

5 Cut out each of the butterfly's wings. Refer to chapter 5 for a review of glass cutting if necessary.

6 Grind the edges of each piece, right up to the edge of the paper pattern, but not beyond.

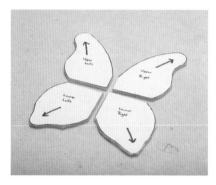

7 Peel off the paper pattern, dry with a towel, and label the pieces of glass with a permanent marker.

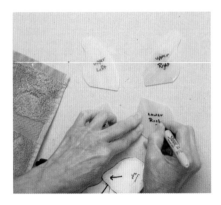

8 Wash the glass pieces with mild detergent and water, rinse, and dry them. Relabel the glass if its label washes off.

9 Once the edges are very dry, wrap copper foil around each piece. Use a 1/4-inch width copper foil with a silver backing. Refer to the "Copper Foiling" section in chapter 6 for proper foiling technique, if necessary.

Start the foil along one of the straight sides, so that the overlap will be anchored into one of the solder seams. This way there will be no chance for the foil to come loose over time.

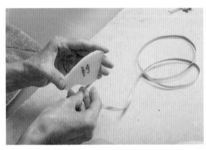

10 Burnish the edges of the foil with a fid. It is important to have the foil well-adhered to the glass for this project, as it may be displayed outdoors and exposed to the elements.

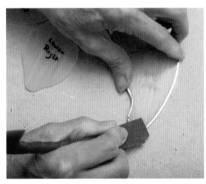

11 Pour a small amount of flux into a cup.

12 Plug in the soldering iron. Set a temperature-control iron at 410 degrees Celsius for soldering on copper foil.

13 Place a 6-inch layout strip on your work surface, holding it in place with two pins.

14 Align the right two wing sections against the straight edge of the layout strip, and pin them into place with a few pins.

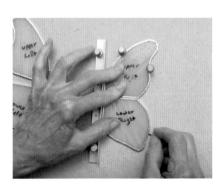

15 Brush flux onto the center seam.

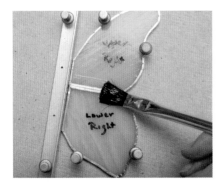

16 Apply a flat layer of solder over the seam.

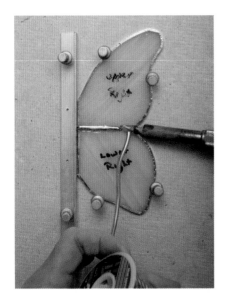

17 Add a little more flux; you do not need to dip the brush back into the flux container. There is plenty of flux remaining on the brush.

18 Add a second coat of solder, making sure it melts into the first coat. It should bead up, giving a nice rounded look to the solder.

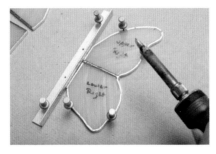

19 Remove the pins and turn the wing over.

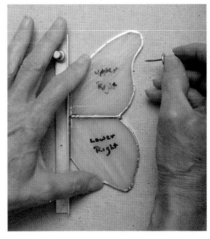

20 Flux the back center seam.

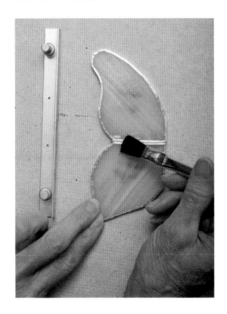

21 Solder the seam.

22 Add a little more flux and add a second coat of solder to get a nice rounded bead.

23 Remove the pins from the layout strip, turn the strip in the opposite direction, and pin it into place. Align the left-wing butterfly pieces against the layout strip and pin them into place.

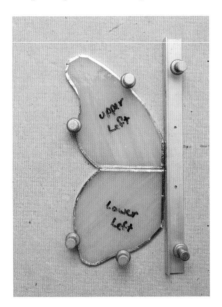

24 Flux and solder the left-wing center seam as you did the right-wing pieces.

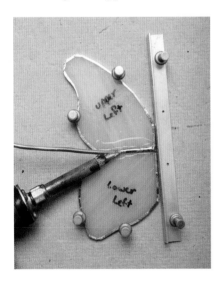

25 Add a little more flux and add a second coat of solder, making sure it melts into the first coat, just as you did with the right-wing pieces.

26 Remove the pins from the wing pieces and turn it over.

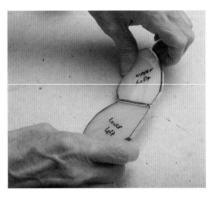

27 Flux and solder the back center seam as you did with the right-wing pieces.

28 Add a little more flux and a second coat of solder, making sure it melts into the first coat.

29 Turn both wing sets right-side up.

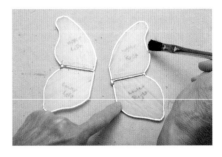

30 Flux around the perimeter of both wing sets.

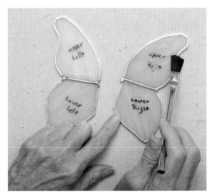

31 Take a tiny bit of solder onto the iron tip. Run the iron tip over the foiled edges, leaving just a bit of solder around the edges of both wings. This process is called *tinning*.

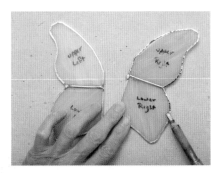

32 Turn over the wing sets and flux the outer edges.

33 Again, add a bit of solder to the iron tip, and slide it around the edges so that the copper foil is covered lightly with solder.

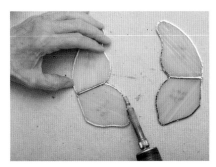

34 Carefully turn the butterfly wing set on edge. Run the iron around the edge of the foil so that solder covers the edges of the wings. Be careful to keep your hand higher than your iron so hot solder does not drip onto your hand. The flux and solder from tinning the top and bottom should be sufficient to cover the edges.

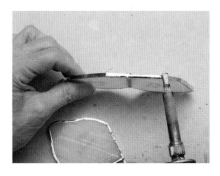

35 Repeat with the second wing set.

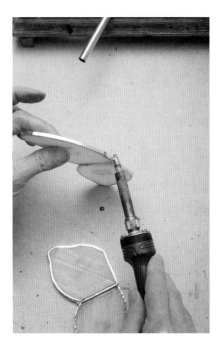

36 Turn both wing sets right-side up.

37 Use Handy Wedges to prop up the wing sets, creating a natural angle for your butterfly. The straight edges should line up to create a center seam.

38 Add a flat coat of solder to the center seam.

39 Make your own twisted wire with a vise, the wire twister, and 20-gauge pretinned copper wire.

- Cut off a 36-inch length of wire.

- Loop it through one end of the wire twister and clamp both ends into the vise.

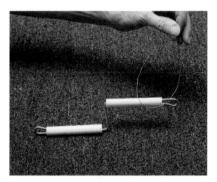

- Turn the wire twister until the wire is twisted to your desired tightness.

- Cut off a 7-inch section for this project and save the rest for future projects.

40 Use the needle-nose pliers to find the center of the twisted wire and bend the wire in half.

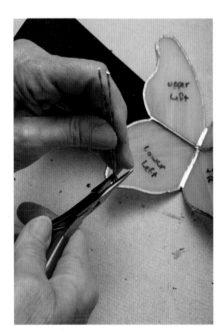

41 Squeeze the bottom of the twisted wire with the pliers.

42 Use the pliers to bend the top of each side of the wire into a loop for the antennae.

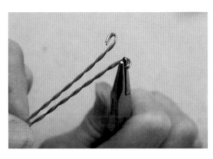

43 Place the antennae at the upper half of the center seam and apply flux to the wire.

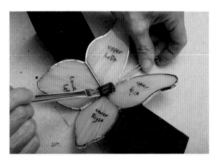

44 Use needle-nose pliers to hold the antennae in place, as heat will travel up the wire.

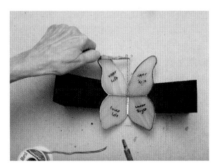

45 Add a bit of solder to your iron and apply it over the twisted wire to hold it in place.

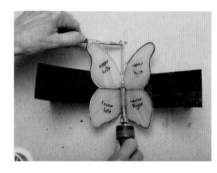

46 Use additional solder to build up the bottom half of the seam.

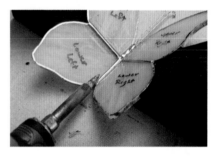

47 Turn the butterfly over.

48 Use your iron to smooth the solder in the center seam.

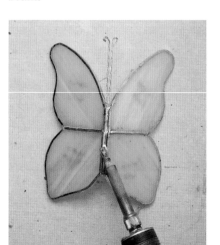

49 Place about 2 1/2 inches of a 36-inch-long brass rod into a vise and bend it to a 45 degree angle.

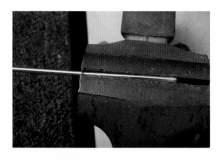

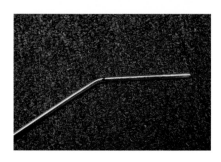

50 Flux the end of the brass rod, from the bend upward.

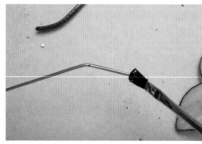

51 Pick up a bit of solder with your iron and slowly tin the entire bent portion. Pretinning the brass rod will allow it to join more easily to the butterfly. Move slowly, as brass takes more heat to adhere solder to it.

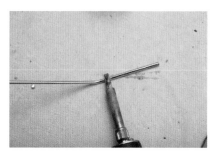

52 Position the bent portion of the rod into the center back seam of the butterfly. It makes it easier to balance if you rest the other end of the rod on your shoulder.

53 Use a bit of solder to tack a few places along the rod to hold it in place.

54 Smooth solder along both sides of the brass rod to fully connect it to the center seam.

55 Turn the butterfly over, separate the ends of the antennae, and bend them into a graceful curve.

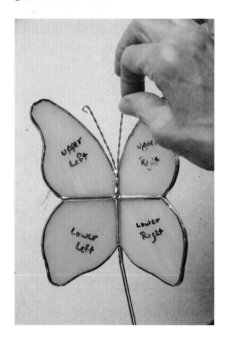

56 Wash the butterfly with mild detergent and water, removing all flux from the edges and seams, as well as the marker writing.

57 Rinse well and dry with a clean towel.

58 Spray both sides of the butterfly with a flux and patina neutralizer. Dry well with a towel.

59 Drip a bit of glass polish on each of the wings. Rub it in with a towel and buff to a beautiful shine. Repeat on the back.

60 Your butterfly stake is ready to watch over your garden. In colder climates be sure to bring your butterfly indoors over the winter months.

LEAD CAME BUTTERFLY GARDEN STAKE

SUPPLY LIST

- ❍ Paper pattern
- ❍ Permanent marker
- ❍ Scissors
- ❍ Rubber cement
- Glass
  - ❍ Approximately ½ square foot or 6x12-inch sheet of glass

  We used Kokomo's Dark Rose/White Opal (26).
- ❍ Safety glasses
- ❍ Bench brush
- ❍ Homasote board or work surface
- ❍ Glass cutter
- ❍ Glass cutting oil
- ❍ Grozing/breaking pliers
- ❍ Running pliers
- ❍ Glass grinder
- ❍ Lead came: 36 inches ⅛-inch U-channel lead
- ❍ Vise
- ❍ Lead cutters
- ❍ Flux and brush
- ❍ Small cup for flux
- ❍ Solder
- ❍ Soldering iron, stand, and wet sponge
- ❍ 6-inch layout strip and pins
- ❍ 2 Handy Wedges
- ❍ Needle-nose pliers

- Wire cutters

- 36 inches of 20 gauge pre-tinned copper wire or 7 inches of twisted 20 gauge pre-tinned copper wire Wire twister tool

- 36-inch tall ⅛-inch brass rod

- Mild detergent

- Wash basins

- Flux and patina neutralizer

- Stained glass polish

- Towels

1 Using regular scissors, cut out the perimeter of the pattern and cut apart the wings. Because this is more of a free-form project, there is no need to use pattern shears to cut out the pattern.

2 Place each pattern piece on the glass, lining up the directional arrows with the color grain or pattern in the glass. Make sure there is space between each pattern piece to separate the glass.

3 Brush rubber cement onto the back of each pattern piece and glue them into place.

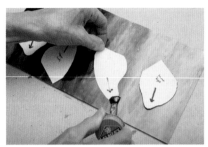

4 Using your glass cutter, score the glass between the pattern pieces and use running pliers to break the glass, separating each piece from the others.

5 Cut out each butterfly wing. Refer to the cutting directions in chapter 5, if necessary.

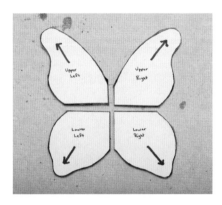

6 Grind the edges of each piece, right up to the edge of the paper pattern but not beyond.

7 Peel off the paper pattern, dry with a towel, and label each piece of glass with permanent marker.

8 Wash the edges of the glass with mild detergent and water, rinse, and dry them.

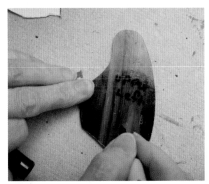

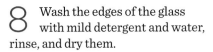

9 If you have a temperature-controlled iron, set it to 360 degrees Celsius. A cooler iron is advised when working with lead came.

10 For this project you will use 1/8-inch U-channel lead, because it is easy to work with and contours nicely to the curves of each butterfly wing. Trim the end of a 36-inch length of this lead came to get a clean 90 degree cut on the end. Remember to trim the lead with the channel facing up. Refer to the lead cutting instructions in chapter 7 for more details, if necessary.

11 Beginning at the corner, slowly wrap each glass piece with the lead, following the contour of the wings. When you reach the beginning again, cut the lead so that it lines up with the first end.

12   Flux the lead joint.

13   Pick up a bit of solder with the tip of your iron and seal the ends of lead together.

14   Add a tack of solder on the top surface and a tack of solder on the bottom surface as well.

15   Repeat with the remaining three wings. Always begin with a clean 90 degree cut on the end of the lead came.

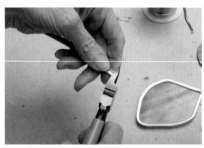

16   Pin the layout strip to your work surface with two pins.

17   Pin the right wings against the layout strip and flux the center seam.

18   Solder the center seam right over the lead.

19   Add a little bit of flux and add a second coat of solder, melting into the first coat. This leaded project has a wider center seam than the Copper Foil Butterfly Garden Stake.

20 Turn over the right wing set and flux the center seam.

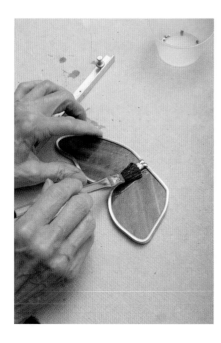

21 Solder over the center lead seam.

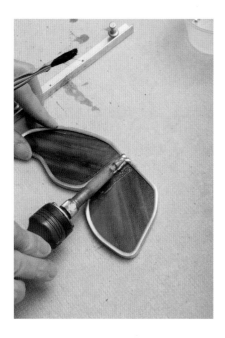

22 Add a little bit of flux and smooth the solder. Add a second coat if necessary.

23 Flip the layout strip to the opposite side and replace the pins.

24 Place the left two wings against the layout strip and pin into position.

25 Flux and solder over the center lead seam.

26 Add a bit of flux and smooth out the center seam with the flat of the iron, adding solder if necessary.

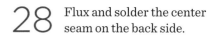

27 Remove the pins and turn over the left wing set.

28 Flux and solder the center seam on the back side.

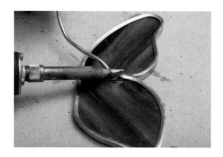

29 Add a little bit of flux. Smooth out the center seam with the flat side of the iron, adding a bit of solder if necessary.

30 Using Handy Wedges, prop the wings up at a natural angle and line up the straight edges to form the center seam.

31 Flux the center seam of the butterfly.

32 Put a flat coat of solder onto the center seam.

33 Refer to the Copper Foil Butterfly Garden Stake and follow the directions for twisting wire. You will need a 7-inch length of twisted wire for the antennae.

34 Place the needle-nose pliers in the center of the twisted wire.

35 Bend the wire in half.

36 Squeeze the bottom of the twisted wire with the pliers.

37 Bend each end of the wire into a loop for the antennae.

38 Place the antennae at the upper half of the center seam and apply flux to the wire.

39 Use needle-nose pliers to hold the antennae in place, as heat will travel up the wire as you solder.

40 Add a bit of solder to your iron and apply it over the twisted wire to hold it in place.

41 Use additional solder to build up the bottom half of the seam.

42 Turn the butterfly over, add flux, and use your iron to smooth the solder in the center seam.

43 Using a vise, bend 2 1/2 inches of a long brass rod to a 45 degree angle for the butterfly's stake.

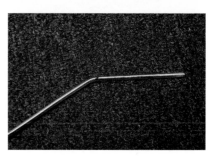

44 Flux the end of the brass rod, from the bend upward.

45 Pick up a bit of solder with your iron and slowly tin the entire bent portion. Lead melts at a much lower temperature than brass, so if the rod is pretinned with solder it will adhere much more easily to the butterfly. Move your iron slowly, as brass takes more heat to adhere solder to it.

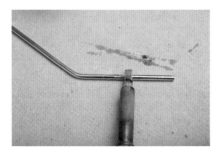

46 Position the bent portion of the rod into the center back seam of the butterfly. It is easier to balance if you rest the other end of the rod on your shoulder.

47 Use tacks of solder in two places along each side of the rod to hold it into place.

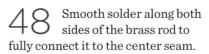

48 Smooth solder along both sides of the brass rod to fully connect it to the center seam.

49 Turn the butterfly over, separate the ends of the antennae, and bend them into a graceful curve.

50 Wash the butterfly with mild detergent and water, removing all flux from the edges and seams, as well as the marker writing.

51 Rinse well and dry with a clean towel.

52 Spray both sides of the butterfly with a flux and patina neutralizer and then dry it with a towel.

53 Drizzle a bit of glass polish onto both sides of the butterfly. Rub it in with a towel, and buff to a beautiful shine.

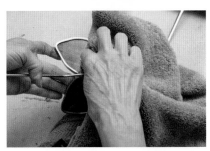

Remember to properly recycle your lead scraps!

The Leaded Butterfly Garden Stake has a different look than the Copper Foiled Butterfly Garden Stake. It is truly a matter of taste as to which style you prefer.

Remember to bring your garden stake indoors during the cold winter months!

9
BEVEL STARS

THE FOLLOWING PROJECTS WILL GIVE YOU A CHANCE TO TRY USING BEVELED GLASS. There is no glass cutting required, although we have provided patterns if you wish to cut glass pieces for these designs instead of using bevels.

The first bevel star project uses 3x5-inch diamond-shaped bevels. We used glue chip bevels in our sample, because we liked the surface texture these bevels exhibit. For a holiday feel, we chose iridized red nuggets. You may wish to use nuggets that complement your home decor.

The second bevel star project is a timeless design. The three-dimensional shape will add a bit of a challenge to your soldering skills, but the outcome is well worth the effort. The teardrop-shaped bevels are available individually or as a bevel cluster kit. This star also looks great when the shapes are cut from clear, textured glass. For added sparkle, try an iridized glass.

Both star projects will be beautiful additions to your holiday decorating, but you may enjoy displaying them year-round.

BEVEL STAR WITH GLASS NUGGETS

SUPPLY LIST

- ○ 6 3x5-inch glue chip diamond bevels OR cut 6 pieces of glass according to pattern (approx. 1 square foot of glass)
- ○ 7 small to medium-size iridized nuggets
- ○ Scissors
- ○ Homasote board or work surface
- ○ Glass grinder
- ○ 96 inches $\frac{7}{32}$-inch silver-backed copper foil
- ○ Small plastic container with lid
- ○ Fid
- ○ Flux and brush
- ○ Small plastic cup for flux
- ○ Solder
- ○ Soldering iron, stand, and wet sponge
- ○ 12 pins
- ○ Needle-nose pliers
- ○ 2 small pre-tinned copper wire rings
- ○ Mild detergent
- ○ Wash and rinse basins

- Flux and patina neutralizer

- Stained glass polish

- Towels

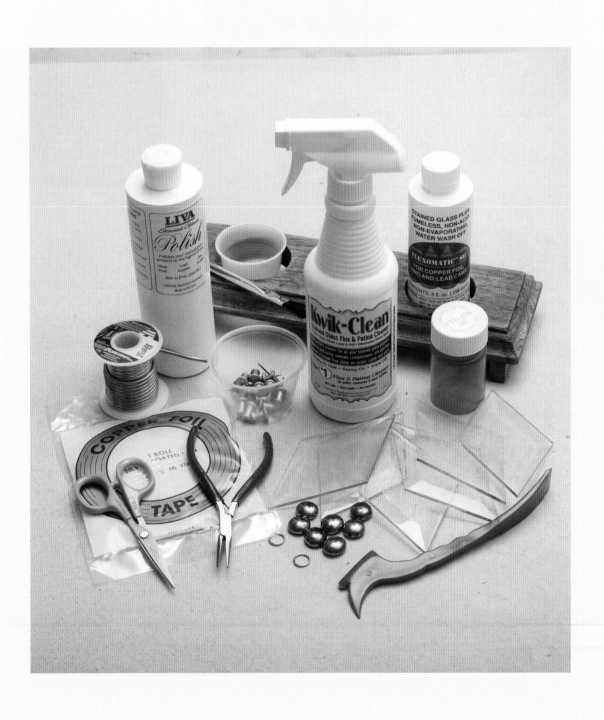

1 Begin this project by preparing the nuggets you have chosen. Lightly grind the edges of all seven nuggets so that the copper foil will adhere well.

2 Wash, rinse, and dry the nuggets well.

3 Apply the copper foil to each nugget, overlapping the foil about a quarter of an inch.

4 Use your fingers to press the foil over the top edge.

PRO TIP

To burnish the foil on nuggets, place them all in a small plastic jar. Close the lid on the jar and shake well for about thirty seconds. Remove the nuggets and see how smooth the foil is!

5 Foil the bevels. Grinding is not necessary, as the edges are smooth and grinding may chip the bevels. Begin the foil along one of the sides and continue around the entire bevel. Overlap the foil a quarter of an inch when you reach the beginning edge. Pinch the corners down first, from one side of the corner, then the other. Slide your fingers down each side to push the foil flat against the glass.

PRO TIP

The overlap of our foil on this bevel was not very tidy, so we used a craft knife to cut away the excess. This will allow the solder to follow the straight lines of the foil.

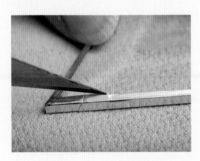

6 Use the fid to burnish the edges of the foil. On the beveled side of the glass, angle the fid to match the angle of the bevel.

7 If you are using sheet glass instead of bevels for this project, you will need to cut, grind, wash, and foil all pieces before assembly.

8 All pieces are now ready to assemble.

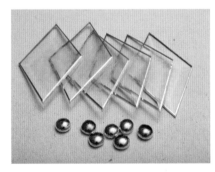

9 Pour a small amount of flux into a small plastic cup.

10 Use a brush to flux the foiled edges of the nuggets.

11 To construct the star, it will go more smoothly if all the components are covered with a small amount of solder. This process is called *tinning*. To tin the nuggets, pick up a small dot of solder with the end of your iron and carefully turn the nugget with a pair of pliers as you apply the solder to the foil. Repeat with the remaining nuggets.

12 Turn over the nuggets and cover any copper foil that is showing with a bit more solder. Be careful, as the nuggets will be hot!

13 Flux the edges of the bevels.

- Pick up a dot of solder with your soldering iron and tin the top side of the bevel.

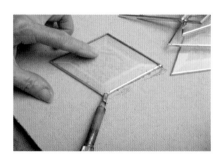

- Turn over the bevel and flux the foil on the back. Pick up a dot of solder and tin the back side of the bevel.

- Pick up the bevel and run the edge of the iron down the side edge of the bevel. Generally, there will be enough solder to cover the side edge without adding more; just be sure no copper is showing.

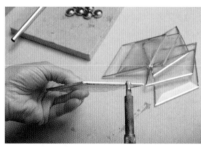

14 Tin the edges of all remaining bevels.

15 Lay out the bevels so that they are all face-up. The angle of these bevels does not allow a perfect connection in the middle, so make sure the bevels line up where their points meet. There will be a small amount of space between each bevel in the interior.

16 Use a pin on the outer two sides of each bevel to keep them in place while soldering.

17 You do not need to add any more flux at this point, as there is plenty of flux from the previous steps.

18 Solder each line from the outside to the center for the first, flat coat of solder.

19 Remove the pins so the star can be moved more easily while soldering.

20 Add another light coating of flux. (No need to redip your brush, as it still contains plenty of flux.)

21 Bead up each solder seam, except in the center. Smooth each line as needed. Rotate the star as you work so that you are always soldering each seam toward yourself. This way, solder will not roll off the edge.

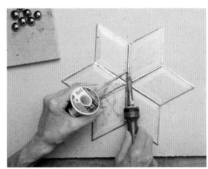

22 After completing the front seams of the star, let the project cool for a few minutes before turning it over. With the wide spaces between the bevels, more solder means more heat, which transfers to the bevels as well.

23 You can see that solder has sealed the gaps between the bevels.

24 Solder the seams on the back, again pulling toward the center. It will generally take less solder to produce a rounded solder bead on the back of the project.

Be careful not to build up too much solder in the center where all six seams come together.

25 When the back seams are completely soldered, turn the star over to the front side.

26 Place a nugget into each of the angles where the bevels meet.

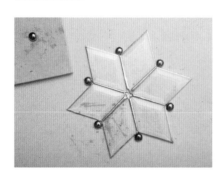

27 Carefully solder each nugget into place at its respective seam.

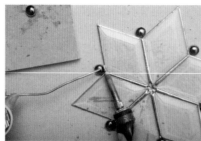

28 Turn the star over.

29 Solder the edge of the nuggets on the back side to connect them into the seams.

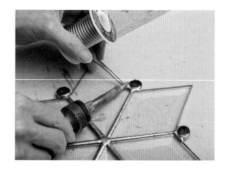

30 Add the hanging rings to your project:

• Brush flux onto the two small rings.

• Place a ring on the outside of a nugget. Use needle-nose pliers to hold the split in the ring over the edge of the star where a nugget meets the bevel.

- Add a bit of solder over the split in the ring. This will seal the split while it anchors the ring to your project.
- Solder the second ring in place on the outer side of the nugget on the opposite side of the same bevel. Again, you will use a dot of solder to cover the split in the ring and attach the ring to the seam between the bevel and the nugget.

31 Turn the star face-up again.

32 Put the last nugget in place, centering it on the star.

33 Add a dot of solder to connect the nugget at each seam, melting into the seam to get a good connection.

34 Wash, rinse, and dry the star.

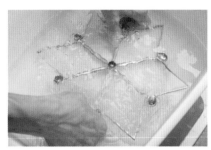

35 Liberally spray both sides of the star with a flux and patina neutralizer.

36 Dry with a clean towel.

37 Drizzle a bit of polish onto both sides of your project. Spread the polish around the glass with a towel.

38 Allow the polish to film up a bit on both sides. Then buff the star to a beautiful shine with a clean part of the towel.

39 Add a length of sturdy ribbon through each of the hooks. Tie the ribbon into a knot and trim the ends.

40 Hang to display for holiday cheer.

- Exquisite Bevel Cluster 343 OR 2 TR04 and 10 TR03 stock bevels OR cut glass according to pattern: 2 larger and 10 smaller teardrops (approximately 1 square foot of glass)

- Homasote board or work surface

- 120 inches ¼-inch silver-backed copper foil

- Fid

- Flux and brush

- Small cup for flux

- Solder

- Soldering iron, stand, and wet sponge

- 8 pins

- Handy Wedge

- Needle-nose pliers

- Wire cutters

- 6 inches 20-gauge pretinned copper wire

- Mild detergent

- Wash and rinse basins

- Flux and patina neutralizer

- Stained glass polish

- Towels

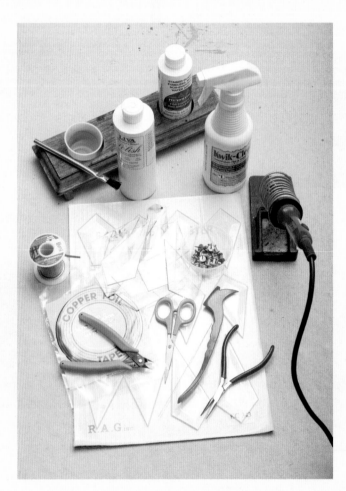

1 Foil each bevel or glass piece, beginning on one of the shorter sides. These sides will be connected in the center seams, so the ends of the foil will be anchored. Refer to the foiling of bevels in the Glue Chip Bevel Star project previously in this chapter, if necessary.

Note: If you choose to use sheet glass for this project instead of bevels, cut, grind, and wash all twelve pieces, then apply the copper foil.

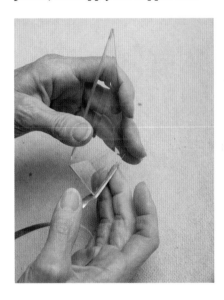

2 Burnish the edges with the fid.

3 Place the two longer bevels on your board, bevel-side up. These bevels should point to the top and bottom. Use two of the smaller bevels to point toward the right and left, also bevel-side up. All four bevels should line up well in the center; the copper foil will form an X.

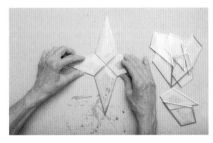

4 Pin each of the bevels in place so they cannot shift out of position.

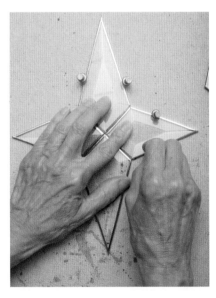

5 Flux the copper foil seams.

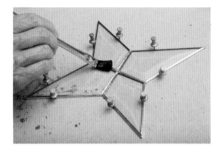

6 Add a flat coat of solder.

7 Remove the pins and turn the star over.

8 Flux the copper foil seams and add a flat coat of solder on the back.

9 Tin the perimeter of the flat star: flux the foil and then add a dot of solder, running it along the back surface of the star.

10 Turn the star over to flux and tin the front.

11 Hold the star to tin the side edges of the bevels. Rotate the star to cover each side, keeping your hand above your iron to avoid dripping hot solder on yourself. No additional flux or solder is generally needed, as there is plenty from tinning the front and back surfaces.

12 Now tin all edges (front, back, and sides) of each remaining bevel. Add the flux, then add a dot of solder to cover all edges of the copper foil.

13   Place the flat star on the work surface, bevel-side up.

14   Take one of the small bevels and center it over a solder seam. The largest point should face outward, so the edges of the bevels line up equally. The bevel side should be facing to the right.

15   Add a tack of solder in two places on each side of this bevel to hold it in place.

16   Take a second bevel and center it over the next seam, again with the beveled side to the right.

17   Add two solder tacks on each side to hold it into place.

18   Take a third bevel and center it over the third seam, with the beveled side to the right. Add two solder tacks on each side to hold it into place.

19   Take a fourth bevel and center it over the final seam, with the beveled side to the right.

20   Add two solder tacks on each side to hold it in place.

21   Now that all four bevels are tacked into place, adjust them so they line up well in the center.

22 Add a few dots of solder to hold the bevels in place in the center where they all meet.

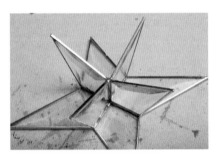

23 Now, holding the star up at an angle, solder each of the seams fully from the center to the outer edge. Each corner has three seams to it, so take care not to miss any.

PRO TIP

Hold the star so that the seam you are soldering is level with the table. The solder will flow evenly if the star remains level.

24 Turn the star over and set it on its four points.

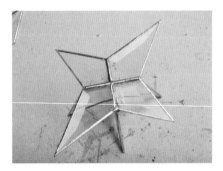

25 Take one of the small bevels and center it over a solder seam. The largest point should face outward, so the edges of the star line up. The bevel side should again be facing to the right.

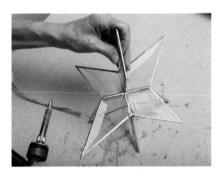

26 Add a dot of solder in two places on each side to hold it in place.

27 Take a second bevel and center it over the next seam, again with the beveled side to the right. Add two solder tacks on each side to hold it into place.

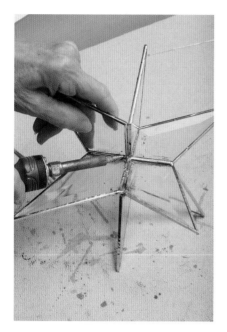

28 Take a third bevel and center it over a third seam, with the beveled side to the right. Add two solder tacks on each side to hold it into place.

29 Take a fourth bevel and center it over the final seam, with the beveled side to the right. Add two solder tacks on each side to hold it into place.

30 Now that all four bevels are tacked into place, adjust them so that they line up well in the center.

31 Add a few dots of solder to hold the bevels in place in the center where they meet.

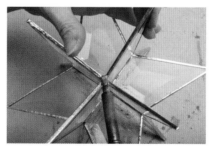

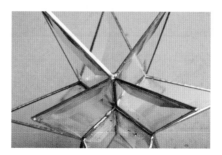

32 Now, holding the star up at an angle, solder each of the seams fully from the center to the outer edge. Again, each corner has three seams to it; take care not to miss any.

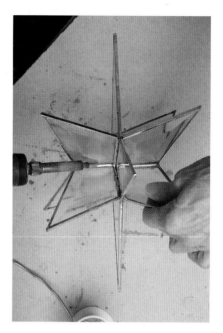

33 Now, at each junction where four bevels come together, add a tack of solder.

34 Review each side to ensure that all seams have been covered, rotating the star to double-check.

35 To make a hook for hanging the star, straighten a small 6-inch length of pretinned copper wire. Fold it in the middle over needle-nose pliers.

36 Twist the wire a few times and open the bottom portion.

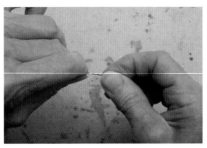

37 Trim the wire so there is about 3/4 inch on either side to attach to the bevel.

38 Turn the star so that one of the longer bevels is facing you. You can prop that end up with a Handy Wedge.

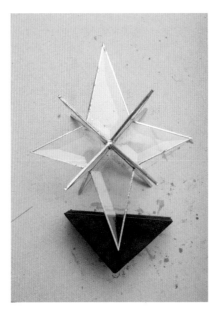

39 Line up the wire so it conforms to the sides of the long bevel point.

40 Flux the wire.

41 Hold the wire with pliers and add a bit of solder to join the wire to the tinned foil.

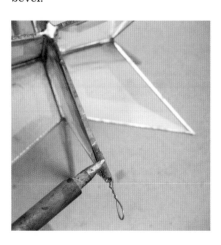

42 Now that it is attached, turn the star on edge and smooth out the solder so it blends in well with the edge of the star. Repeat these steps to anchor the other end of the wire on the other side of the bevel.

43 Wash, rinse, and dry the star.

PRO TIP

Use an old toothbrush to get all the flux out of the tight corners.

44 Liberally spray the star with a flux and patina neutralizer, getting into all the nooks and crannies.

45 Dry with a clean towel.

46 Drizzle a bit of polish onto all sides of the star. Spread the polish around the glass.

47 Allow the polish to film up a bit on all sides. Then, buff the star to a beautiful shine with a clean part of the towel.

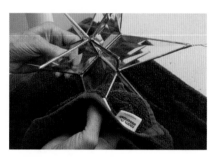

You now have a beautiful star to display for holiday cheer!

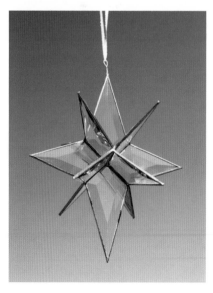

APPROXIMATELY 6-8 HOURS

10
COPPER FOIL CANDLEHOLDER

IF YOU HAVE FOLLOWED THE SEQUENCE OF PROJECTS UP TO THIS POINT, YOU WILL HAVE GAINED SOME SKILLS IN WORKING WITH THREE-DIMENSIONAL DESIGNS.

This candleholder will combine the processes of making copper foil panels with creating an upright dimensional object. A few new pieces of equipment will be introduced to bring the panels together more easily.

The example shown here has a more detailed design for the front panel and simpler designs for the three remaining sides. You may wish to use the front panel design on the back panel, or even all four sides. This will change the recommended amounts of glass suggested for the project, so please allow for that adjustment.

The candleholder shown in the example was created with warm colors, a prairie-style design, and a copper patina. When the candle inside was lit, this project took on a special glow!

SUPPLY LIST

- ○ Paper pack: oak tag, carbon paper, tracing paper

  Patterns

  - ○ 1 copy of the front panel

  - ○ 3 copies of the side panels, each on a different color paper

  - ○ 1 copy of the base

- ○ Drawing tools: pencil and permanent marker

- ○ Ruler

- ○ Masking tape

- ○ Scissors

- ○ Pattern shears for foil

- ○ Rubber cement

  Glass

  - ○ 1 square foot clear texture

  - ○ 1 square foot another clear texture

  - ○ ½ square foot dominant color

  - ○ ½ square foot complementary color

  - ○ 3 (¾-inch-square) clear bevels

  We used Oceanside's Clear Vecchio (S100V) and Oceanside's Clear Crystal Ice (S100GG) for the clear textures and Wissmach's Red/Amber Streaky (W11LL) and Oceanside's Medium Amber Water Glass (S1108W) for the colors.

- ○ Safety glasses

(continued on next page)

- ⦾ Bench brush
- ⦾ Homasote board or work surface
- ⦾ Glass cutter
- ⦾ Glass cutting oil
- ⦾ Grozing/breaking pliers
- ⦾ Running pliers
- ⦾ Glass grinder
- ⦾ $7/32$-inch copper-backed copper foil
- ⦾ Fid
- ⦾ Craft knife
- ⦾ Flux and brush
- ⦾ Small cup for flux
- ⦾ Solder
- ⦾ Soldering iron, stand, and wet sponge
- ⦾ Layout strips and pins
- ⦾ The Professional Boxer
- ⦾ 2 Handy Wedges
- ⦾ Mild detergent
- ⦾ Wash basins
- ⦾ Newspaper
- ⦾ Flux and patina neutralizer
- ⦾ Protective gloves
- ⦾ Copper patina
- ⦾ Small sponge
- ⦾ Stained glass polish
- ⦾ Towels

1 Assemble a paper pack of oak tag, carbon paper, and tracing paper. Trace one pattern for the front of the candleholder and one for the remaining sides. For the three sides, photocopy the pattern onto three different colors of paper. It is important that each side fits together well, so using different colors of paper will help keep each panel separate.

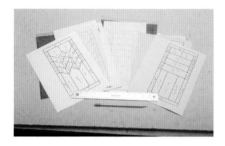

2 Cut the perimeter of the patterns with regular scissors.

3 Cut the interior of the patterns with pattern shears for foil.

4 After cutting out each side, separate the pattern pieces based on the glass that they will be glued onto. There will be three pattern pieces that can be discarded, as the center of the design uses three 3/4-inch bevels.

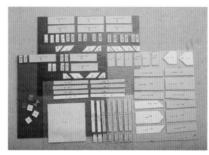

5 Lay out each pattern piece onto their respective glasses, following the directional arrows to capture the swirl or pattern in the glass.

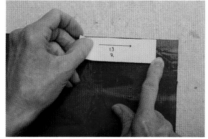

6 Glue down each pattern piece, leaving enough room to separate the glass and cut out each piece.

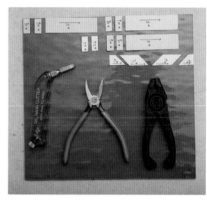

7 Score and remove the excess glass.

8 Separate the individual pieces.

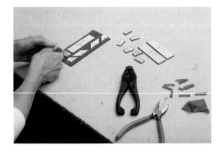

9 Cut out each piece. Refer to chapter 5 for cutting instructions, if necessary.

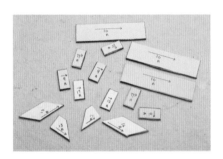

10 Grind the edges of each piece, up to the edge of the pattern paper but not beyond. Do not grind the bevels, as it may chip their edges.

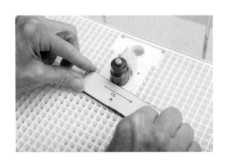

11 Prior to washing, remove the paper and label each piece so that each side will be distinguishable once all papers are removed. Label the glass with green pattern pieces with the letter G and their number.

12 Wash, rinse, and dry each piece. If the letters or numbers wash off, be sure to rewrite them immediately.

Here the amber water glass pieces are shown from each side of the candleholder: ground, labeled, washed, rinsed, and dried.

13 Foil each piece with 7/32-inch copper-backed copper foil, so the foil backing matches the copper patina that will be added later.

14 Foil and burnish each piece of glass and the 3/4-inch bevels, referring to the "Copper Foiling" section in chapter 6 for proper technique, if necessary.

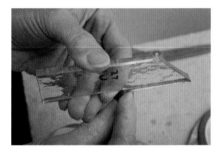

15 Lay out each panel to ensure all pieces are together with their appropriate side. You can label the as follows: W (white), G (green), B (blue), and P (purple) (from the color copies).

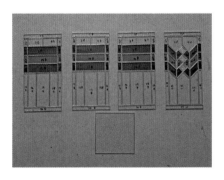

16 To set up the front panel of the candleholder, make a jig over the oak tag pattern using layout strips and a 30°-60°-90° tool to keep the panel in line with perfect right angles.

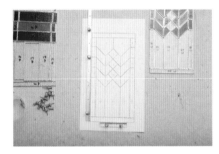

17 Put all the glass pieces and the bevels into place.

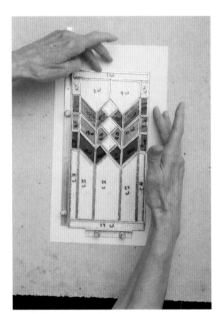

18 Pin in the right and top sides with layout strips, making sure they are also square.

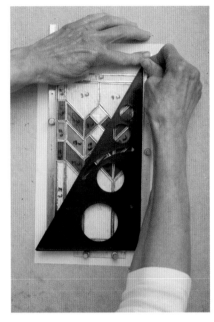

Note: If there is some extra space between your pieces, adjust them so they split the space between a few seams, rather than having a gap in one area.

19 Set up a second jig for one of the side panels, the same way as was done for the front panel. Each of the side panels will be soldered in this jig to ensure they are the same size.

20 Be sure to measure the height and width of the two jigs to make sure they are identical in size.

21 In the jigs, flux each of the foil seams.

22 Tack solder each piece for the front panel within the jig. Refer to the "Soldering" section in chapter 6 for proper soldering techniques, if necessary.

23 Tack solder each piece for the side panel within the jig.

24 Remove one end of each jig and slide out the tacked panels.

25 In the jig for the side panel, build one of the other sides and replace the bottom layout strip, measuring to ensure the height is still the same.

26 Flux the foil seams and tack solder this side. Then, remove the end of the jig again and slide out this second side panel.

27 Repeat with the third side panel so that it is also tack soldered together.

28 Now, dismantle the jigs. You should have all four panels individually tack soldered.

29 Now you are ready to solder the seams of each of the four panels.

30 Begin with one panel. Flat solder each seam on the front.

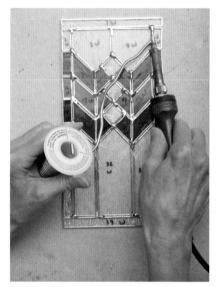

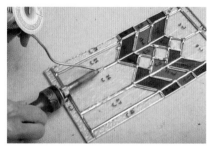

31 Add a little more flux and add the beaded coat of solder.

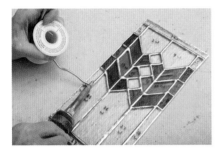

32 Flux and tin the top, bottom, and side edges with a light coating of solder.

33 Turn the panel over. Flux each seam on the back.

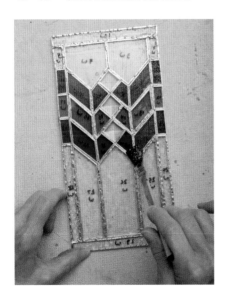

34 Flat solder the back side of the panel.

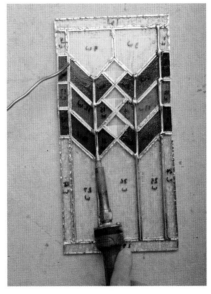

35 Run the flux brush over the solder seams and add the beaded coat of solder.

36 Tin the top, bottom, and side edges with a light coating of solder.

37 Repeat the soldering process for the remaining panels.

38 Flux and tin all edges of the bottom square piece.

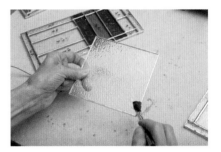

39 Before constructing the candleholder, make sure all four panels and the bottom piece have been fully soldered and their edges have been tinned.

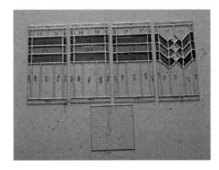

40 To assemble the candleholder, you will use a Handy Wedge and the Professional Boxer to aid in the building process.

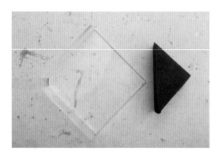

41 Use the Handy Wedge and the Professional Boxer to line up two sides in the right-angle corner. Line up the panels so that the inside edges just touch. Solder will later fill in the groove between the outer edges, creating stability.

42 Add a tack of solder on the top and near the bottom to hold these two sides together.

43 Remove the wedge and turn the structure to add another side into the right angle of the box. Again, line it up so that the inside edges are just touching, leaving an open groove to fill with solder later.

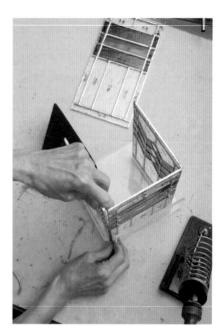

44 Replace the wedge into the corner and tack solder the top and near the bottom to join that side to the others.

45 Remove the wedge and turn the structure again, adding the final side into the corner with the right angle.

46 Replace the wedge into the corner and tack solder the top and near the bottom.

47 Turn the structure, bringing the final open seam into the right angle and tack solder the top and bottom into place.

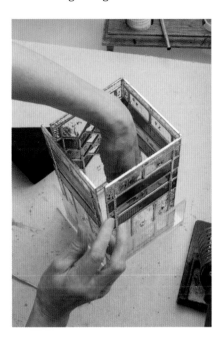

48 Turn the box upside down and place the bottom glass into position so that the textured side is inside the box.

49 Tack solder the bottom into place, adding a few tacks for each side.

50 Turn the box onto one side and flat solder to fill in each of the seams along the base.

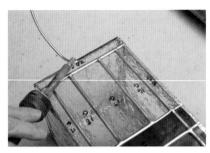

51 Turn the candleholder and repeat until all four sides have been soldered. Add a bit of solder to smooth each seam if necessary. These seams should be smooth, but not necessarily beaded up like the seams on a flat panel.

52 Flux the inside along the bottom seams.

53 Use the soldering iron to clean up any solder drips on the inside edge. Because the foil is not exposed here, and it is difficult to maneuver with the iron, you will not necessarily be making a solid seam on the inside. The exterior seam is strong enough to keep the box together.

54 Use two Handy Wedges to prop up the candleholder on an edge.

55 Flux the interior seam.

56 Flat solder the interior seam.

57 Add a bit more flux, and add a second, beaded coat of solder to this seam.

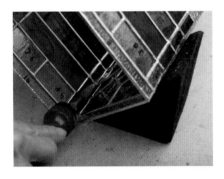

58 Turn the candleholder 90 degrees to reveal another interior seam.

59 Flux, flat solder, flux, and add the beaded coat of solder to this seam.

60 Repeat with each of the final two seams.

61 Stuff the insides of the candleholder with newspaper while working on the outer seams. If any solder drips through, it will land on the newspaper rather than dropping onto another panel of glass, which could potentially crack.

62 Use the Handy Wedges to position the candleholder so that a seam is on the top edge, level with your work surface.

63 Flux this outer seam.

64 Turn down the soldering iron's temperature control just a bit so that solder is less likely to melt through the seam.

65 Add solder along the outer seam and work slowly with the iron to smooth the seam, filling in all the space between the outer edges of glass.

66 Repeat with the remaining outer seams on each corner of the box.

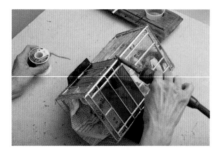

67 Turn the candleholder upright and flux the top edge.

68 Take a bit of solder and add it to the top edge to give it a rounded look.

69 Remove the newspaper.

70 Thoroughly wash, rinse, and dry. Take care to scrub off all the marker numbers on the glass.

71 Spray liberally, both inside and outside, with a flux and patina neutralizer.

72 Dry with a towel.

73 Cover your work surface with newspaper and put on a pair of protective gloves for applying patina.

74 Pour some copper patina onto a small sponge and apply it to all the seams of the candleholder, inside and out.

75 Gently wash and rinse. Pat dry.

76 Spray liberally with a flux and patina neutralizer; dry well.

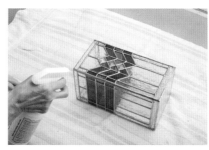

77 Drizzle the project with glass polish and spread around the inside and outside of the project with a towel. Let the polish film up.

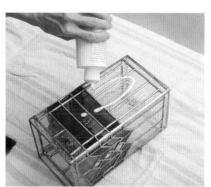

78 Buff to a beautiful shine with a clean towel.

You can use either a traditional candle or a flameless candle in your candleholder. Enjoy the warm feeling that candlelight can bring to a room!

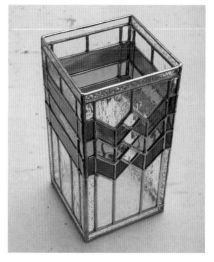

11
TIFFANY-STYLE PANEL LAMPSHADE

CREATING A LAMPSHADE CAN BE A CROWNING ACHIEVEMENT IN YOUR STAINED GLASS JOURNEY. While at first glance, this may look like a daunting task, think of the project in steps. You will be creating six identical panels using the same skills you learned when making the copper foil panel in chapter 6.

The key to making a beautiful Tiffany-style lampshade is to accurately cut, grind, and solder each panel of the lamp so it is exactly like the other sides. Be consistent; you have the skills to take on this challenge!

Think about where you will display your finished lamp. You may wish to choose glass colors that will complement the decor in the room where the lamp will be placed.

A new technique that you will learn during this project is wiring the top and bottom of the shade to reinforce the seams, providing strength and stability to the finished product. You will add a cap to the top of your shade so that it will be ready to place on a purchased or repurposed lamp base.

Electrical wiring is not discussed in this book, and should not be attempted by anyone without appropriate experience.

When completed, your beautiful lamp will brighten any room. Incandescent bulbs were traditionally used in stained glass lamps, but you may wish to experiment with some of the more energy efficient bulbs available today.

SUPPLY LIST

- ○ Paper pack: oak tag, carbon paper, tracing paper
- ○ 6 copies of the pattern each printed on a different color paper
- ○ Drawing tools: pencil and permanent marker
- ○ Masking tape
- ○ Scissors
- ○ Pattern shears for foil
- ○ Rubber cement
- Glass
  - ○ 3–4 square feet for the background
  - ○ 1 square foot each of three complementary colors

  We used Oceanside's Clear/White Corsica (S600081) for the background. For the complementary colors, we used Oceanside's Aqua/Rose/White/Clear Corsica (S603483), Kokomo's Two Blues Opal (K123), and Kokomo's Solid Purple Opalume (K3D).

- ○ Safety glasses
- ○ Bench brush
- ○ Homasote board or work surface
- ○ Glass cutter
- ○ Glass cutting oil

(continued on next page)

- ○ Grozing/breaking pliers
- ○ Running pliers
- ○ Glass grinder
- ○ $\frac{7}{32}$-inch black-backed copper foil
- ○ Fid
- ○ Craft knife
- ○ Flux and brush
- ○ Small cup for flux
- ○ Solder
- ○ Soldering iron, stand, and wet sponge
- ○ Layout strips and pins
- ○ Vinyl electrical tape
- ○ Needle-nose pliers
- ○ Wire cutters
- ○ Approximately 66″ of 20-gauge pre-tinned copper wire
- ○ 3½-inch vented vase cap
- ○ Steel wool
- ○ 2 Handy Wedges
- ○ Lamp support wedge
- ○ Mild detergent
- ○ Wash basins
- ○ Newspaper
- ○ Flux and patina neutralizer
- ○ Protective gloves
- ○ Black patina for lead and solder
- ○ Small sponge
- ○ Stained glass polish
- ○ Towels

Note: When making a lamp it is very important to choose glass that is not too transparent, so that the light fixture inside is not visible. However, glass selection should allow enough light to come through so that the lamp is also functional.

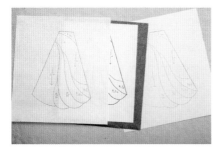

1 As in the other projects, begin with a paper pack of oak tag, carbon, pattern, and tracing paper.

2 Trace the pattern.

3 Draw in numbers for each piece, letters to color-code, and directional arrows for the texture or pattern in the glass.

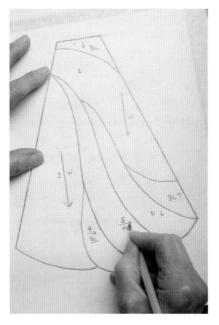

4 Take the original pattern and photocopy it onto six different colors of paper that will be the patterns for each of the six sides of the lamp. It is important that each side fits together well, so using different colors will help keep each panel separate.

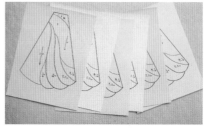

5 Begin by cutting the perimeter of each pattern with regular scissors.

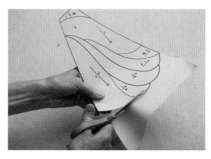

6 Use pattern shears to cut out the pattern pieces.

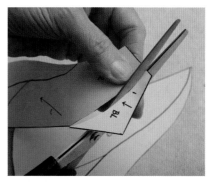

7 Lay out the pattern pieces on the appropriate glass, according to the directional arrows. Glue down the pattern pieces with rubber cement.

8 Separate the glass into manageable pieces.

9 Proceed with one panel at a time from this point forward, so that the pieces from the different sides do not get mixed up. You are working with the panel designated by blue pattern pieces.

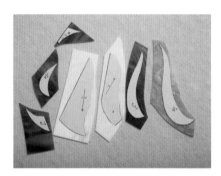

10 Cut out each piece of glass. Refer to chapter 5 for a review of successful cutting, if necessary.

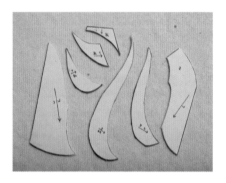

11 Grind each piece of glass.

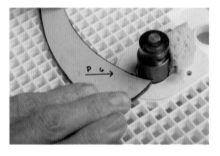

12 Peel off the pattern, wash, rinse, and dry each piece. Write the pattern number and a letter B (blue) on each piece.

13 Foil each piece. Use 7/32-inch black-backed copper foil, as later you will add a black patina to the lamp. Refer to the "Foiling" section in chapter 6 for proper foiling techniques.

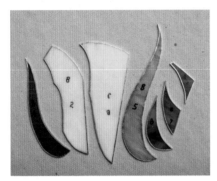

14 If there are any places that the foil overlap is off-center, trim the excess with a craft knife.

15 Continue by cutting, grinding, marking, washing, and foiling the glass pieces from the remaining five sides. Be careful to keep the pieces from each panel together so they do not get mixed up with the others.

16 Take the oak tag copy of the pattern and create a jig to use for soldering each of the individual panels. Use pins to hold layout strips in place for the top, left, and right sides of the panel. Using a jig in this manner will ensure that each panel will have the identical angles and will come together well when all six panels are assembled to form the lamp.

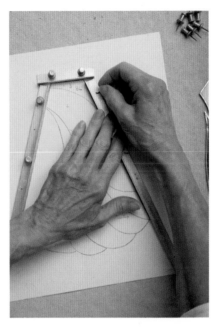

17 Assemble the first panel inside the jig.

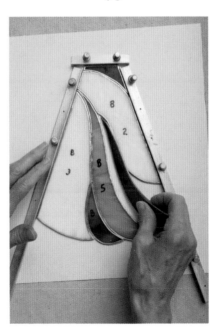

18 Make sure the bottom of each piece lines up with the pattern, and pin those pieces into place.

19 Now the panel is ready to solder.

20 In the jig, flux each foil seam.

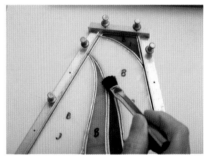

21 Tack solder each piece within the jig. Refer to the "Soldering" section in chapter 6 for proper soldering technique, if necessary.

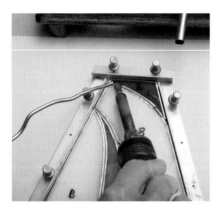

22 Remove that panel, and build the next one in the same jig. Flux and tack solder this panel in the jig.

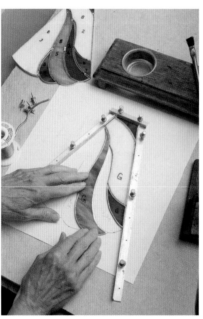

23 Repeat until all six panels are tack soldered and then remove the jig.

24 Beginning with one of the panels, flat solder each seam on the front side.

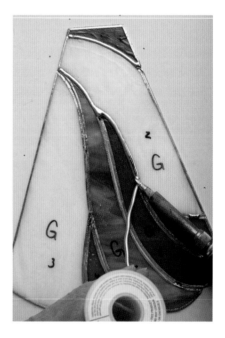

25 Add a small bit of flux to the solder seams, and add the beaded coat of solder.

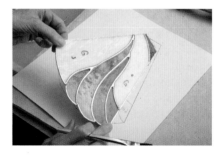

26 Tin the top and bottom edges of this panel. No need to tin the sides.

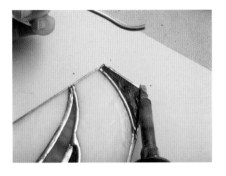

27 Turn the panel over.

28 Flux each seam on the back of the panel.

29 Flat solder the back side of the panel.

30 Add a small amount of flux to the solder seams and add the beaded coat of solder.

31 Tin the top and bottom edges of this panel. There is no need to tin the sides.

32 Repeat all soldering steps for the remaining five panels.

33 Wash, rinse, and dry all six panels.

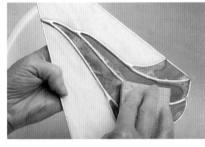

34 Arrange the panels so that the top and bottom edges line up, with about an eighth of an inch of space between each panel.

35 Tape each vertical seam with vinyl electrical tape, leaving a bit of space open at the top and bottom for a solder tack. Press down firmly to ensure the tape is well-adhered.

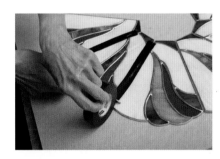

36 Place a line of tape near the top, connecting all the panels together in a semicircle. Leave a tab of tape extending over the edge of the first panel and finish that line just a bit short of the last panel.

37 Repeat with a line of tape near the bottom edge of the glass, again leaving a tab of tape that extends over the first edge and then stopping short on the last panel.

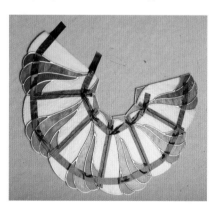

38 Grasp the top edges of the lamp and gently lift it until the edges meet.

39 Take the tabs of tape and connect them to the adjoining panel.

40 Measure the top of the lamp, from a flat side to a flat side; it should measure about 3 inches in diameter. This will be important for fitting the cap later.

41 Tack solder the panels together near the top of each seam. Flux first, then add a dot of solder to hold the panels together.

42 Use your fingers to move the panels into position so they line up well before tack soldering.

43 Flux near the bottom edge of each seam. Align the panels with your fingers, and tack solder them into place.

44 Repeat until all seams are tacked.

45 Wire the top of the lamp. Begin by estimating about how much wire is needed, leaving a little extra to work with. Cut off the amount needed from the spool.

46 Flux the top edge of the lamp.

47 Flux the entire length of the wire.

48 Begin the wire in the middle of a panel and tack solder the end into place.

49 Use a pair of needle-nose pliers to help bend the wire along the contour of the lamp.

50 Add solder tacks to hold the wire to the top edge of the lampshade at the seams.

51 Continue around the top edges, adding solder tacks every inch or so.

52 When you reach the beginning again, cut the wire so that it does not overlap, and tack it into place.

53 Add a line of solder the entire way around the wire so that it becomes fully connected to the top of the lamp.

54 Prepare the cap by using a piece of steel wool to scour the surface.

55 Flux the entire surface of the cap.

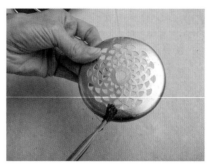

56 Tin the cap by adding some solder and spreading it around until the whole surface has a light coating of solder, including the edge. A little bit of solder goes a long way in this step. The key to tinning is to use a lot of flux and a lot of heat.

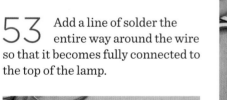

57 Use a pair of needle-nose pliers to hold up the cap while tinning the edges.

58 Place the cap on top of the lamp. Adjust the cap so that it is level and touches each seam.

59 Add a tack of solder where each seam meets the cap.

60 Lay the lamp onto its side. Use Handy Wedges to keep the lamp from moving. The inside seam to be soldered should lay flat against the work surface.

61 Flux the seam and add a flat coat of solder.

62 Flux again and add the beaded coat of solder.

63 Rotate the lamp so that the next seam is flat against the work surface.

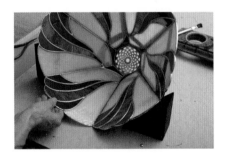

64 Repeat the sequence of adding flux, a flat coat of solder, a bit more flux, and a beaded coat of solder for each seam.

65 Turn the lamp upright and gently remove all the tape.

66 Use caution when removing the vertical tape lines so that the copper foil does not come loose from the glass.

67 Set up the lamp support wedge and pin it into place so it cannot move.

68 Prop up the lamp so that one seam is parallel to your work surface. The bottom edge of the lamp goes against the lamp support wedge so the cap is toward you. Use Handy Wedges along the bottom to help hold it in place.

69 Flux the seam and add the flat coat of solder.

70 You may want to turn the iron down a bit so that the chance of solder melting through to the other side is lessened. You may also add some crushed newspaper inside to prevent hot solder from dripping onto an interior piece of glass.

71 Add a small amount of flux over your solder seam.

72 Add the beaded coat of solder and smooth it again if necessary. Be sure to maintain a good connection to the cap.

73 Rotate the lamp to the next seam. Repeat the sequence of adding flux, a flat coat of solder, a bit more flux, and a beaded coat of solder for each remaining seam.

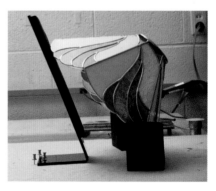

74 Smooth out the solder on each seam, if necessary.

75 Turn the lamp so the bottom edge is facing up and use Handy Wedges to hold it in place.

76 Estimate how much wire the bottom edge will require and cut that length from the spool.

77 You may wish to stretch the wire with a vise to straighten out any bends or kinks.

78 Flux the bottom edge of the lamp.

79 Flux the entire length of the wire.

80 Begin the wire midway along one of the longer glass pieces.

81 Tack the end of the wire on the rim of the glass with a dot of solder.

82 Use a craft knife to help bend the wire into the crevices along the contour of the glass. Continue adding tacks of solder every inch or so as you move along the edge.

83 When you reach the beginning point, cut the end of the wire so it lines up flush with the start of the wire and tack it into place.

84 Now cover the entire wire with solder so that it blends into the bottom edge of the lamp.

85 Lay the edge of the lamp onto the work surface and go over the outside seams and inside seams to clean up anywhere there is excess solder, blending the wire into the seam.

86 Gently wash the inside and outside of the lampshade. Be sure to wash off all flux and any residue left from the electrical tape.

87 Rinse and dry the inside and outside of the shade.

88 Cover your work surface with newspaper.

89 Spray the inside and outside liberally with a flux and patina neutralizer.

90 Thoroughly dry the shade with a towel.

91 Put on protective gloves before applying the patina.

92 Pour a bit of black patina onto a clean sponge. Apply the sponge to all the solder lines on the inside of the shade. Thoroughly rub in the patina along every seam. Also apply the patina to the lower edge of the shade.

93 Turn the lamp right-side up and patina the cap as well as the solder seams on the outside of the lamp. Continue until there is no more silver showing.

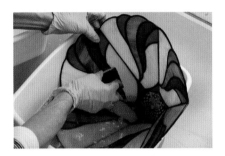

94 Gently wash the shade with mild detergent and water.

95 Rinse the shade and pat it dry.

96 Spray the inside and outside liberally with a flux and patina neutralizer.

97 Dry with a clean towel.

98 Drizzle a bit of polish on the outside of the lamp and spread it around with a towel. Allow the polish to film up.

99 Then drizzle a bit of polish on the inside of the lamp and spread it around with a towel. Allow it to film up.

100 After a few minutes, take a clean towel and buff the inside and outside of the lamp to a beautiful shine.

Your lampshade is now ready to display.

Choose a lamp base that will complement your beautiful new shade, sit back, and enjoy your hard work!

12
BASIC STAINED GLASS REPAIR TECHNIQUES

AS YOU CONTINUE TO CREATE BEAUTIFUL STAINED GLASS PROJECTS,
IT IS INEVITABLE THAT YOU WILL ENCOUNTER A CRACKED OR BROKEN
PIECE OF GLASS. Whether the broken piece is in something you made or is brought
to you by a friend who needs to have it fixed, you are now up to the challenge of
completing a minor repair. One or two broken pieces in a stained glass panel are quite
manageable if you follow these step-by-step instructions. More difficult repairs or
badly damaged stained glass pieces may need to be referred to a professional.

1　In this panel, one broken piece of glass is marked.

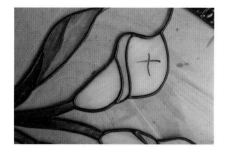

2　To remove this broken piece, you need to break it further into smaller pieces. Score the glass multiple times across the piece in one direction.

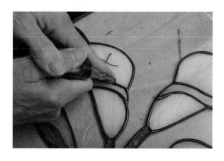

3　Turn it and score across the glass in another direction, making a crosshatch of scores. Make sure your scores go right up to the solder lines.

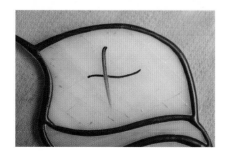

4　Turn the panel over and support it on either side of the broken piece.

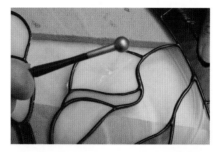

5　Use the balled end of a stick cutter to tap the glass until it breaks out in the center. Use a gentle touch so as to not accidentally break adjoining glass pieces.

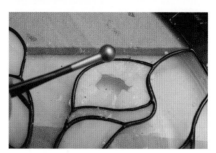

6　Use steel wool to clean the oxidation and patina from the solder seams surrounding the broken piece.

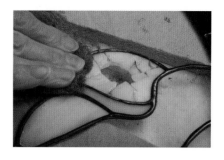

7　Flux the seams surrounding the broken piece of glass that you will be removing.

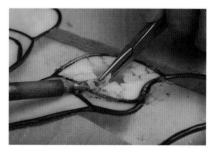

8　Use the soldering iron to melt the solder seam and loosen the adhesive on the foil of the broken pieces. Take care not to pull the foil from the adjoining intact pieces.

9 Use needle-nose pliers to pull glass pieces out as the heat loosens them.

10 Once the glass pieces are all removed, you will need to remove the foil.

11 Use the needle-nose pliers to grasp one end of the loose foil and place the iron between that and the intact foil pieces to melt the solder that is holding them together. Continue around the perimeter until all of the foil from that piece has come loose.

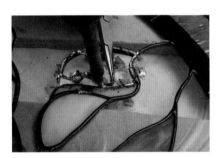

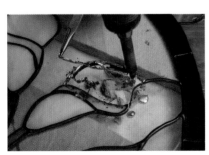

12 Take the iron around the perimeter to clean up any excess solder.

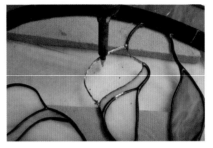

13 Now you will need to make a pattern for the replacement piece of glass.

14 Turn the panel over so the front side is facing up again.

15 Place a small piece of paper underneath the opening in the panel. Use a pencil to trace the outline of the piece, taking care to keep the paper from moving.

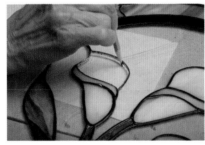

16 Draw an arrow on the pattern piece to indicate which direction the color grain should run.

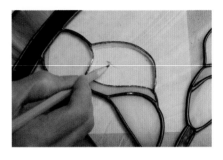

17 Cut out the pattern with regular scissors.

18 Glue the pattern onto the glass, taking care to note the direction of the texture or pattern in the glass.

19 Cut out the piece of glass and grind it. Check to make sure it fits well in place. Do some touch-up grinding if necessary.

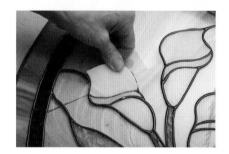

20 Wash, rinse, and dry the glass.

21 Foil the piece of glass with the same kind of foil used in the original panel.

22 Use a few coins to prop up the piece of glass so that it is at the same level as the glass in the rest of the panel.

23 Flux the seams.

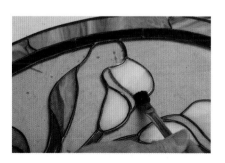

24 Add a coat of flat solder around the piece.

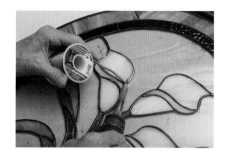

25 Use steel wool to clean old patina or oxidation from any seams that adjoin and do not easily accept the new solder.

26 Brush on a bit of flux and add the beaded coat of solder.

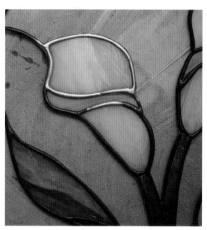

27 Turn the panel over. You no longer need the coins to prop up the glass.

28 Add flux to the back seams.

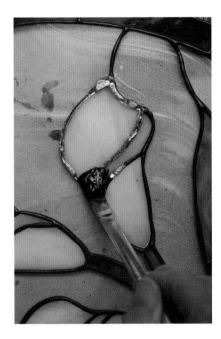

29 Use your iron to distribute any solder that has come through from the front side.

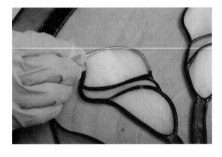

30 Flux again, and add more solder for the beaded coat, if necessary.

31 Spot clean the area with a soapy sponge.

32 Spray liberally with a flux and patina neutralizer and dry with a towel.

33 Put on protective gloves and then add a bit of patina to a sponge and rub over the solder seams in that area to match the patina on the rest of the panel.

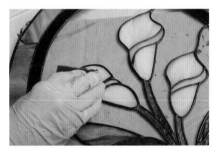

34 Spot clean that area with a sponge, mild detergent, and water.

35 Spray that area with a flux and patina neutralizer and dry it off.

36 Turn over the panel and repeat the process to patina, clean, neutralize, and dry.

37 Polish the entire piece. Drizzle a bit of polish on the glass and solder seams and spread it around. Let that side film up while you add polish to the other side.

38 Turn the panel over and drizzle a bit of polish on the panel. Spread it around with a towel and let it film up.

39 Buff both sides of the panel with a clean towel until it has a beautiful shine.

40 A soft-bristled brush can help to remove old or excess polish from solder seams.

41 The repaired panel looks as good as new!

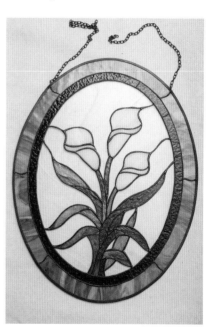

13
PATTERNS

INCLUDED IN THIS CHAPTER ARE THE PATTERNS FOR PRACTICING
GLASS CUTTING AS WELL AS THE PATTERNS FOR THE PROJECTS
IN THIS BOOK. There are also additional patterns for you to perfect your new
stained glass making skills.

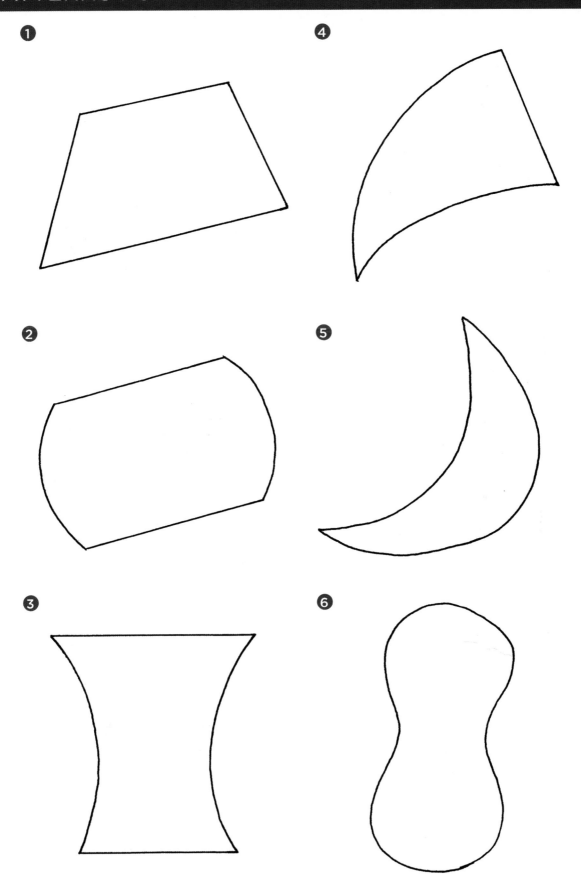

❶

❷

❸

❹

❺

❻

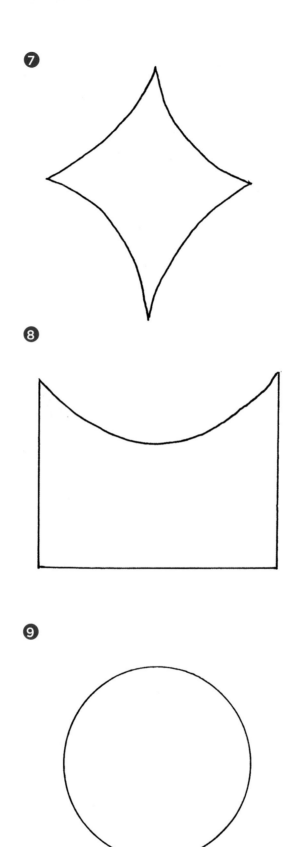

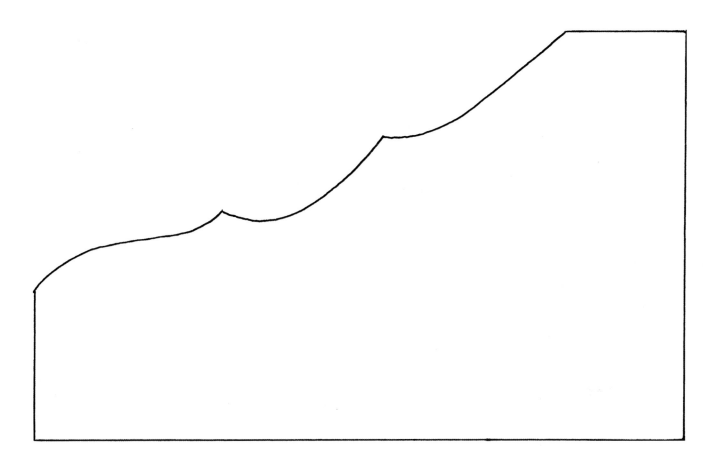

Enlarge pattern 175% for a 12x12-inch panel.

LEAD CAME TRADITIONAL PANEL

Enlarge pattern 166% for a 10x14-inch panel.

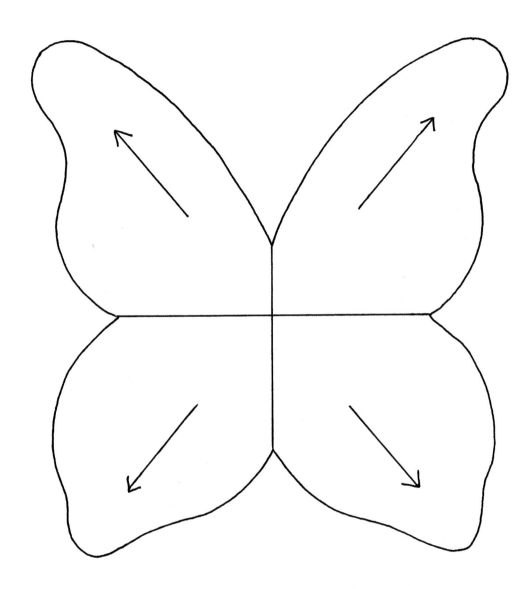

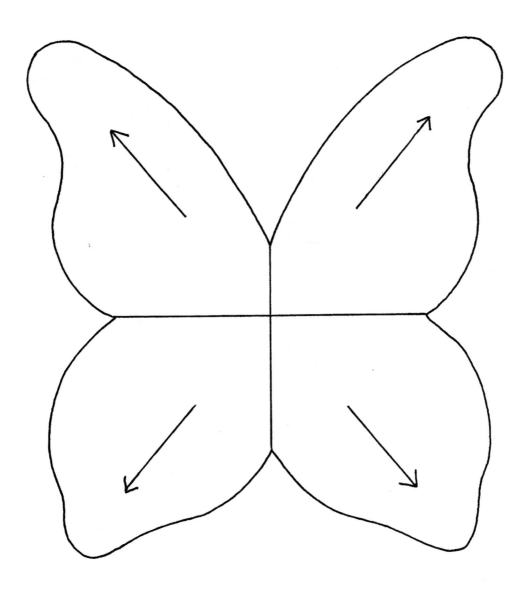

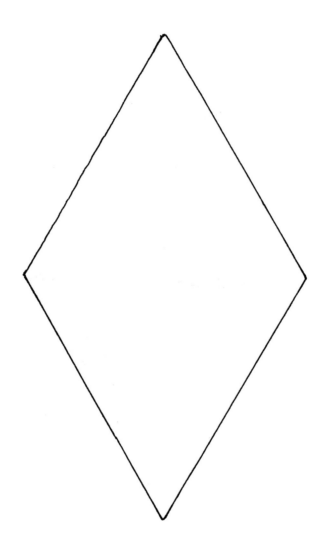

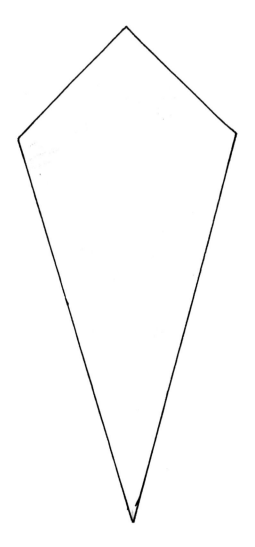

Cut 2 pieces of this size pattern.

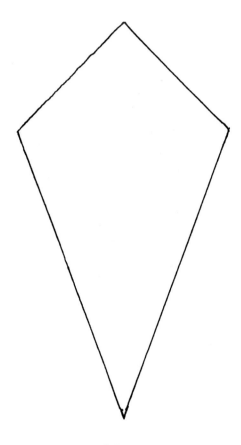

Cut 10 pieces of this size pattern.

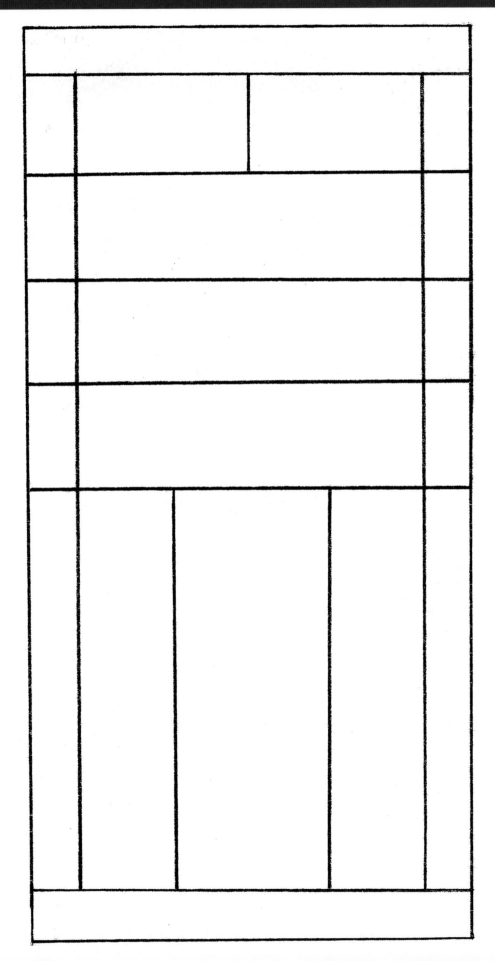

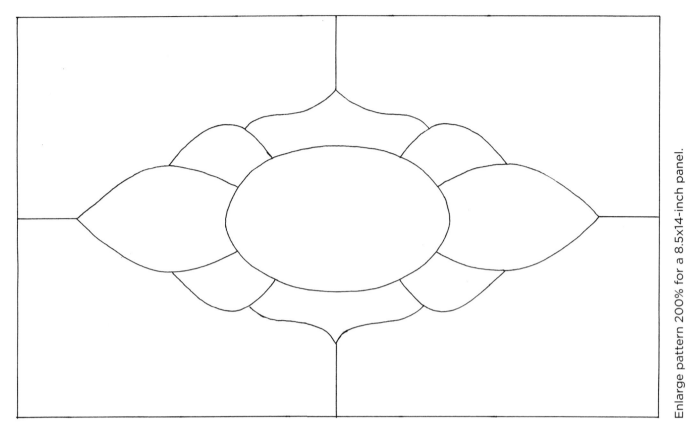

Enlarge pattern 200% for a 8.5x14-inch panel.

This pattern is for a 6-sided lamp.

Enlarge pattern 135% for a 8.75-inch high panel.

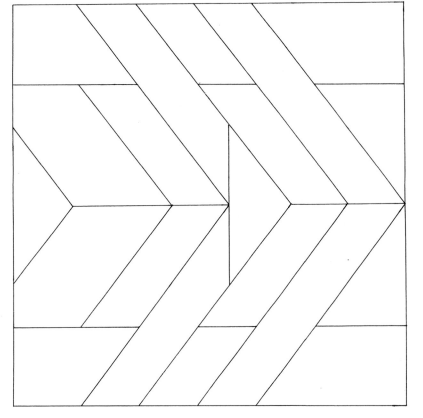

Enlarge pattern 235% for a 10x10-inch panel.

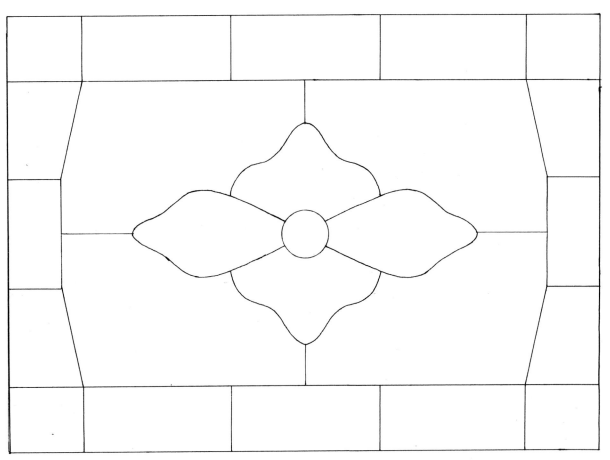

Enlarge pattern 220% for a 10x14-inch panel.

ACKNOWLEDGMENTS

FOR MANY YEARS, the original version of *Basic Stained Glass Making* has been a great resource for all of us at Rainbow Vision Stained Glass. It was a pleasant surprise when I was asked to revise the book and update the projects. Many thanks to Mark Allison and Judith Schnell of Stackpole Books for the opportunity to work on this with them.

My deepest appreciation to my daughter, Katie. She has worked side-by-side with me through every step in creating the revised book, and she has designed each of the new projects presented. Without her keen artistic ability and organizational skills, the revised book would not have as polished an appearance.

A very special thank you to Alan Wycheck of Alan Wycheck Photography in Harrisburg, Pennsylvania. His eye for capturing an image from just the right angle, with exactly the right lighting, is exceptional. I appreciate his dedication and expertise while collaborating on this project with us.

The staff at Rainbow Vision has been great while I have been working toward completion of this book. Lee Summers, Jan McKelvey, Lou Ann Benedict, Melissa Flood, and, again, Katie Haunstein have all been very helpful and supportive. They have been wonderful with hands-on assistance and as advisors whenever I needed their help. They are the best!

And last, but never least, my gratefulness to my husband Jim and my family and friends. Your complete support throughout the revision process was wonderful. Thank you.

—Lynn Haunstein

RESOURCES

Rainbow Vision Stained Glass, LLC
3105 Walnut Street
Harrisburg, PA 17109
www.rainbowvisionsg.com

Rainbow Vision offers a large array of stained glass and fused glass classes and carries a complete line of tools, supplies, equipment, and sheet glass from a variety of manufacturers. Custom design and stained glass panel construction as well as glass repairs are also offered.

Retailers of Art Glass and Supplies (RAGS)
www.stainedglassretailers.com

RAGS is a nonprofit organization of retail store owners with members from across the United States and around the world. Use the "Store Locater" function on the website to find a retail stained glass store near you!

Stained Glass Association of America (SGAA)
255 Pratt Street
Buffalo, NY 14204
www.stainedglass.org

SGAA is a professional trade association working to elevate the art of stained glass through classes and product development. For more than a century, SGAA has maintained historical archives, provided a wealth of information to its members, and continues to advance the craft of stained glass.

Alan Wycheck Photography
331 South Front St.
Harrisburg, PA 17104
alan@alanwycheckphoto.com
www.alanwycheckphoto.com

GLASS MANUFACTURERS IN THE UNITED STATES

Bullseye Glass Company
3722 SE 21stAve.
Portland, OR 97202
www.bullseyeglass.com

Kokomo Opalescent Glass
1310 S. Market St.
Kokomo, IN 46902
www.kog.com

Oceanside Glass & Tile
5858 Edison Place
Carlsbad, CA 92008
www.glasstile.com

Paul Wissmach Glass Company, Inc.
420 Stephens St.
Paden City, WV 26159
www.wissmachglass.com

Youghiogheny Opalescent Glass Company
300 S. 1st St.
Connellsville, PA 15425
www.youghioghenyglass.com

Also available from Stackpole Books

Beyond Basic Stained Glass Making

40 Great Stained Glass Projects

Making Stained Glass Boxes

Making Stained Glass Lamps

Making Tiffany Lamps

Basic Glass Fusing

40 Great Glass Fusing Projects